20
LINEAR WALKS
in
LAKELAND

Paddy Dillon

^A**QUESTA**Guide

ISBN 1 898808 14 7

ADVICE TO READERS

Readers are advised that while the author had made every effort
to ensure the accuracy of this guidebook, changes can occur
which may affect the contents. The Publishers would welcome
notes of any changes you find.

Maps:
The maps accompanying the walks in this book are purely
diagrammatic, based on out-of-date maps, and no substitute for
modern Ordnance Survey Outdoor Leisure Maps

Published by
Questa Publishing, 27 Camwood, Bamber Bridge, Preston, Lancashire
PR5 8LA
and printed by
Carnmor Print, 95/97 London Road, Preston, Lancashire PR1 4BA

Contents

Introduction

For many people a car may be a convenience, but it can also be a liability. While it's true that many walkers who visit the Lake District bring their cars with them, it's also true that you simply don't need a car to explore the place on foot. Having a car generally limits you to completing circular walks. Not having a car leaves you free to walk from dale to dale, over and along entire ranges of fells, because there's no need to return to retrieve a vehicle. Walkers who can read timetables and grasp the opportunity to use public transport creatively can enjoy lovely linear walks through the Lake District.

True, with a car you can drive at leisure and enjoy a certain measure of freedom, but you're tied to returning to the car at some point. If you're tired and soaked to the skin, driving can be unpleasant after a walk. There may be small parking spaces in remote areas, but if they're full, then you have to keep moving and maybe abandon the walk. Popular car parks are inevitably pay-and-display, and even then they're not immune from the attention of thieves.

Using public transport will necessarily tie you to starting and finishing at a bus stop, train station or ferry landing, but you don't have to return to the place where you started. Instead, you can keep walking and finish far from where you started, having enjoyed an immense variety of scenery along the way. Of course, you need to have up-to-date timetables and pace yourself so that you don't miss the last bus. It's simply a matter of being organised; of being able to read public transport schedules alongside walking routes and figure out how to tie everything together.

Public transport revolves largely around bus services in the Lake District. The main operator is Stagecoach in Cumbria, and during the busy half of the year they produce a useful magazine-style listing of popular bus services. Trains are useful for reaching the Lake District, but they don't penetrate further than Penrith, Kendal, Windermere or around the Cumbria coast. It's worth knowing about unusual forms of transport, such as Post Buses, or the delightful Ravenglass & Eskdale Railway, and don't forget the wonderful ferry services on some of the larger lakes. There's no reason why you shouldn't combine a train journey with a bus journey, or a bus journey with a ferry journey.

Be aware of the current availability of services, of seasonal variations, school buses, changes at weekends, or particularly limited services. In the Lake District, there are a number of ways to access public transport information. You can ask at Tourist Information Centres, where they should have details and may have timetables you can take away with you. A comprehensive timetable book called 'Getting Around Cumbria & The Lake District' contains even the most obscure little services and is generally published every six months. It's possible to phone Traveline on 0870 608 2 608 and obtain details of anything that moves, whether on rails, roads or water.

Another online source is the Journey Planner operated by Cumbria County Council at www.cumbria.gov.uk/travel. The important thing is to know what's available before you go striding over the fells. In one instance, if you miss a bus you might get another in 10 minutes, while in another case you might have to wait 10 months! If you carry a comprehensive set of timetables with you, then you'll always know what your options are if you decide to alter your route. Maybe you can descend to a different place than you originally intended, but in the sure and certain knowledge that a bus will be along to collect you.

Of course, it's possible to bring a car to the Lake District and park it at one end of a walk, then complete a linear walk, and use public transport to travel back and retrieve the car. If considering this approach, it could make more sense to park your car at the end of a walk, then travel to the start, so that you can walk back over the tops to your vehicle at your leisure.

My own experience of using public transport in the Lake District offers an insight into how flexible the system can be. Summer or winter, I can leave home as early as 0600 and there's a bus that will get me home by midnight. That leaves a good 18 hours to fill with travelling to a starting point, walking over the fells to a finishing point, maybe getting a bus to some other place for another short walk, or to a town for an evening meal, maybe even a late movie, before heading home. In other words, a very full and varied day out! There are bus tickets that offer unlimited transport for one day, four days, a week or a month, giving progressively better and better value for money.

Using public transport frees you from the cost of driving a vehicle around the Lake District, of fuelling it, paying parking fees, etc. Sitting on top of an open-top double-decker is an exhilarating experience that gives you a completely new view of the Lakes! Leaving the driver to do the driving leaves you free to observe the scenery, or if you're tired, to nod off in a corner and take a nap.

As a user of public transport you can enjoy a couple of pints in a Lakeland hostelry after your walk, but not too much, or you'll be barred from the bus!

Natural bases for walking holidays include towns such as Windermere, Ambleside and Keswick, or villages such as Grasmere, which are on the main bus routes and offer easy connections with other services. The more remote western and eastern parts of the Lake District aren't as well served by public transport, but don't neglect them on that account, just take a more careful look at the timetables to spot opportunities to enjoy long walks over the fells.

Do you want the Lake District to be a National Park or a National Car Park?

Think Green! – and leave the car at home. Use public transport.

I
Wray - Windermere Shore - Lakeside

Windermere is England's longest lake and occasionally it occurs to someone to walk the length of it. Unfortunately, most of the busy eastern shore is bounded by roads, but there are a number of pleasant paths and tracks that can be linked along the western shore. The bus running from Ambleside to Hawkshead allows walkers to get close to Wray, and from there it's easy to reach the wooded shoreline. A short walk leads to Ferry House, where a year-round ferry offers a rapid crossing to Bowness. Continuing southwards it's possible to reach Lakeside, where from April until the end of October, a fleet of fine steamboats offer sailings back to Ambleside. Combining a lake walk with a lake cruise is the best way to explore Windermere.

Total distance: 11¾ miles (19 kilometres)
Height gain: 575 feet (175 metres)
Start: At the turning for Wray: GR363016
Finish: At the steamboat berth at Lakeside:
GR378875

1. Use the bus from Ambleside to Hawkshead and get off before Hawkshead at a junction with the B5286 road and a minor road for Wray and Wray Castle. Walk along the Wray road to reach a splendid gatehouse giving access to the grounds around Wray Castle. Just alongside is a lesser gateway where a narrow, but clear track leads down to the shore of Windermere at High Wray Bay. If you follow the access road to Wray Castle, you can turn right at the end of the road and follow the lakeshore to High Wray Bay.

2. Simply continue along the lakeshore track, sometimes in mixed woodland and sometimes with more of a view. Pass a car park at a road-end and continue along a broader track

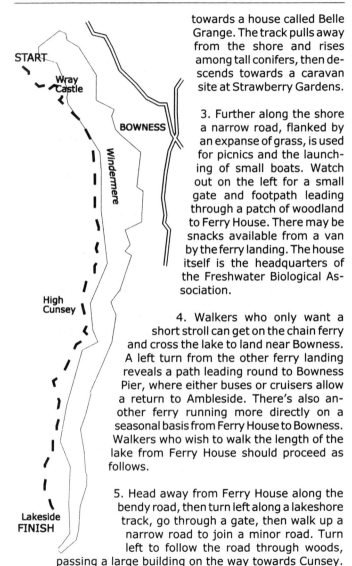

START

Wray Castle

BOWNESS

Windermere

High Cunsey

Lakeside FINISH

towards a house called Belle Grange. The track pulls away from the shore and rises among tall conifers, then descends towards a caravan site at Strawberry Gardens.

3. Further along the shore a narrow road, flanked by an expanse of grass, is used for picnics and the launching of small boats. Watch out on the left for a small gate and footpath leading through a patch of woodland to Ferry House. There may be snacks available from a van by the ferry landing. The house itself is the headquarters of the Freshwater Biological Association.

4. Walkers who only want a short stroll can get on the chain ferry and cross the lake to land near Bowness. A left turn from the other ferry landing reveals a path leading round to Bowness Pier, where either buses or cruisers allow a return to Ambleside. There's also another ferry running more directly on a seasonal basis from Ferry House to Bowness. Walkers who wish to walk the length of the lake from Ferry House should proceed as follows.

5. Head away from Ferry House along the bendy road, then turn left along a lakeshore track, go through a gate, then walk up a narrow road to join a minor road. Turn left to follow the road through woods, passing a large building on the way towards Cunsey.
6. A path signposted on the left leads quickly down to the

lakeshore. Bear in mind that in wet weather the low-lying path can flood. Cross a small footbridge, then a larger footbridge over Cunsey Beck and turn around a wooded point at Rawlinson Nab. There's a viewpoint bench among the oaks. Follow the path along the shore and up steps to reach the road.

7. Turn left to follow the road, which is again in woodlands and gradually pulls away from the shore, climbing steeply uphill for a short way. Watch out for a public footpath sign on the left at the top of the road. The path runs through mixed woodland and is usually fenced on either side. It leads down to a boathouse and a house beside the lake. Regain the shore beyond the house and pass an area where pheasants are reared.

8. The shore path is narrow and tree roots and boulders can be slippery. Simply follow the path along the wooded shore, largely walking among beech trees. When a fence is reached there's a sudden turn up to the road again.

9. Turn left to follow the road past the entrance to the multi-activity YMCA Lakeside Centre. Watch carefully to spot a short length of path alongside the road, sometimes on the right and sometimes on the left. Use these to avoid walking along the road, especially if there is a lot of traffic.

10. Follow the road through High Stott Park and keep left at road junctions in Low Stott Park. Note the carefully restored old Bobbin Mill at Low Stott Park, which can be visited provided you keep an eye on the time. Remember there is a ferry or bus to be caught at the end of the walk.

11. The road quickly reaches the Lakeside Hotel. Attractions abound when you turn left. During the summer there are regular ferry sailings to Bowness and Ambleside, as well as steam trains running along a short length of line to nearby Haverthwaite. There's the interesting Aquarium of the Lakes too, but it's quite likely that an extra day would be needed to take everything on board and apportion time to study everything properly.

12. In the winter, when there are no sailings from Lakeside,

you can walk another mile (1.5 kilometres) along the road to link with bus services at Newby Bridge. Buses run from here to Bowness, Ambleside and Kendal, as well as in the other direction to Ulverston and Barrow.

Windermere Steamboats

The Swan, Teal and Tern used to be real steamboats, but they were all converted to diesel. In their heyday they were part of the Furness Railway Company, as was the Lakeside & Haverthwaite Steam Railway, and indeed the Gondola on Coniston Water was part of the same concern. There can be no better way to close this walk than to enjoy a leisurely cruise along the whole length of Windermere, reviewing the course of the walk while taking in fine views of the surrounding countryside. Fine fells are seen on the final run to Ambleside.

Journey to the Office

In the 19th century, Barrow Ironmaster Henry Schneider enjoyed a notable journey to work. His wife didn't like Barrow-in-Furness, so they lived in a hotel at Bowness-on-Windermere. Each workday morning, a butler carried Henry Schneider's breakfast down to the shore of Windermere, where the steamboat 'Esperance' was waiting. This craft sailed to southwards to Lakeside, where a special train continued the journey to Barrow. The whole journey was reversed in the evening.

Stott Park Bobbin Mill

The well-wooded shores of Windermere are anything but natural. The woodlands you walk through were once managed exclusively as coppices. Teams of men worked throughout the area, cutting trees almost to their roots, encouraging the growth of several new shoots. Each slender trunk would be cut again and again, so that local charcoal burners, rural blast furnaces and bobbin mills had a constant supply of wood. There is little to remind visitors of charcoal burning or iron production in the area, but Stott Park Bobbin Mill offers an insight into what was once an important local industry, fed by the surrounding coppice woods. Wooden bobbins were once produced in vast numbers and transported to cotton mills. These days, the coppices tend to be rather wild, straggly and overgrown, though in some places they are trimmed back at intervals.

2
Windermere – High Street – Patterdale

Most walkers think Windermere town is a long way from the high fells, and in a sense they are right. Sometimes it's interesting to see how the town gives way to the countryside, and how the lowlands give way to the high fells, and this walk manages to do all these things. Just above Windermere Station is the celebrated viewpoint of Orrest Head, and it's possible to link paths and tracks to continue over the High Street range, descending to distant Patterdale for a bus. Really tough walkers, with an eye on their timetables, could even continue from High Street to Pooley Bridge by referring to Walk 3. In summer there are buses from Patterdale back over Kirkstone Pass to Windermere, but it's also possible to travel around the fells by way of Penrith and Keswick to return to Windermere.

Total distance: 15½ miles (25 kilometres)
Height gain: 3,705 feet (1,130 metres)
Start: Windermere Station: GR414986
Finish: Patterdale: GR395159

1. Leave Windermere Station, where buses and trains connect, and cross the main road outside to see a sign pointing the way to Orrest Head. Simply follow a narrow road that winds up a wooded slope to a blacksmith's house. Beyond the house, any paths continuing up the wooded slope lead to a gate giving access to Orrest Head. The path leads above the trees and there's a surprisingly extensive view taking in the length of the lake and range upon range of fine fells. The view was described by Wordsworth as 'a universe of Nature's fairest forms', and by Wainwright as 'a pageant of loveliness, a glorious panorama'.

2. Looking roughly northwards from Orrest Head you can see

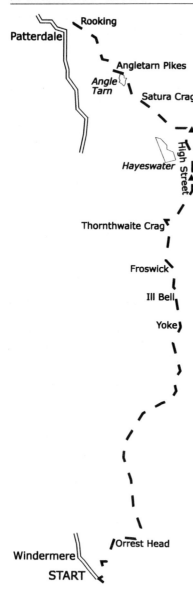

a whitewashed farm called Causeway. Walk towards it along a path, which is then deflected to the right of the farm to join a minor road. Turn right along the road and pass the farm called Near Orrest, then turn left at a crossroads. Turn left at the next road junction, then turn right onto Dubbs Road.

3. Dubbs Road is a broad and clear old road that rises gently to Dubbs Reservoir, continuing to a junction with the rough and stony track known as the Garburn Road above Troutbeck. Keep right and climb gently uphill past old slate spoil heaps, then climb a little more steeply. The old road is enclosed until it runs close to the top of the Garburn Pass around 1,475 feet (450 metres).

4. Turn left off the Garburn Road and cross squelchy ground to gain a firmer footing as you head north towards the higher fells. The path wriggles up the slope and there's a ladder stile over a drystone wall. Climb up to a cairn and the true summit cairn on Yoke is

seen ahead at 2,309 feet (706 metres). Looking further northwards you can see a line of shapely fells, and you cross them all.

5. Follow the path down from Yoke, following the broad and grassy crest, to cross a gap where there's a lot of overtrodden peat. A steep and stony path leads up to the summit of Ill Bell, which is crowned by a series of pepperpot cairns. The highest of these cairns stands at 2,476 feet (757 metres). Views are remarkably extensive and seem to be getting better all the time.

6. A steep and stony path drops downhill and levels out on a grassy ridge. Climb uphill to reach the summit cairn on Froswick at 2,359 feet (720 metres). A descent leads to another gap, then as you climb there are fine views back along the ridge already traversed. At a junction of paths, it's worth keeping to the left to reach the prominent pillar-cairn on top of Thornthwaite Crag. This stands at 2,569 feet (784 metres) and there's a rather attractive view back towards Windermere.

7. A broad, clear path swings in an arc across a gentle gap towards High Street. When it reaches a ruined drystone wall, either continue along the path, or follow the course of the wall to the summit trig point on High Street at 2,718 feet (828 metres). Although views are remarkably extensive, the broad expanse of grass and sedge tend to make everything look rather distant. If time can be spared, then scout around the edges to peer down into deeply-cut dales. Both the path and the wall run down to a gap at the Straits of Riggindale.

8. If you are bursting with energy and wish to traverse the whole of the High Street range, then switch to Walk 3 and continue all the way to Pooley Bridge. Lesser mortals should keep to the left while climbing from the Straits of Riggindale and cut across the slopes of The Knott. It's also possible to follow the course of the wall over the summit of The Knott, as both the wall and the path join on the descent towards Patterdale.

9. Walk down the path and roughly contour across the slopes of Rest Dodd. The path wriggles across the hummocky ground

at the top of Satura Crag, then drops down to Angle Tarn. The tarn is dotted with little islands and is quite attractive. The path climbs a little beyond the tarn, then descends with fine views of Patterdale before being drawn into a little valley.

10. The path runs just below the gap of Boardale Hause, and as there are other paths intersecting at this point, be sure to take the path slanting north-west down across the fellside in the direction of Ullswater. This path splits into parallel courses and either one will suffice for the descent. They join together beside a stand of trees and reach a gate at the bottom of the slope.

11. Go through the gate and follow a narrow road across Goldrill Bridge. Turn right along the main A592 road to enter Patterdale village. The White Lion and Post Office are immediately to hand, with the Patterdale Hotel just beyond. Just along the road are bus stops on either side of the road. If there's time to spare, it's also possible to continue to Glenridding. Summer bus services allow a rapid return over Kirkstone Pass to Windermere, otherwise it's a long way back round via Penrith and Keswick.

Patterdale

Patterdale is named after St. Patrick, and although the man is nearly always associated with Ireland, tradition holds that he was once shipwrecked in the Duddon estuary and walked all the way across the Lake District. It is said that he baptised 5,000 people at the head of Ullswater. At the side of the road, near the head of the lake, is a stone well that is usually dry. This is St. Patrick's Well: Patterdale's Parish Church is also dedicated to St. Patrick.

3
Kirkstone Pass - High Street - Pooley Bridge

The ancient Roman road that runs across the top of High Street is a natural candidate for a linear walk. Although it could be traced from the valley bottom around Troutbeck, then followed most of the way to Penrith, it's maybe better to gain a bit of height and start at the Kirkstone Pass Inn, then leave the lower part of the route near Pooley Bridge. This allows walkers the chance to tie in with summer bus services over Kirkstone Pass, as well as all-year-round buses at Pooley Bridge. There is an option for an early descent from High Street.

Total distance: 18¾ miles (30 kilometres)
Height gain: 2,790 feet (850 metres)
Start: Kirkstone Pass Inn: GR402081
Finish: Pooley Bridge: GR472245

1. A summer bus service runs over the Kirkstone Pass, giving walkers a leg-up to 1,500 feet (455 metres) to start this walk. The Kirkstone Pass Inn was built in 1496 to serve travellers on the road. Just beside the inn a stile gives access to a path climbing away from the road. Cross another stile further uphill and simply follow a path alongside a drystone wall to reach a cairn on top of St. Raven's Edge.

2. Swing left and walk alongside the wall as it crosses a slightly boggy dip. The wall leads up onto the broad, hummocky top of Caudale Moor. The summit is close to a junction of ruined walls at 2,502 feet (764 metres). Be warned that the top of this fell can be a confusing place in mist, and indeed, the whole walk has some rather featureless stretches in poor visibility.

3. A ruined wall drops eastwards and it's necessary to grapple

15

with rocks on the way down to a gap at
Threshthwaite Mouth. Climb a steep
and stony slope to follow a path to a
prominent pillar-cairn on top of
Thornthwaite Crag. This stands at 2,569
feet (784 metres) and there's a rather
attractive view of Windermere.

FINISH

Pooley
Bridge

Barton
Fell

4. A broad, clear path swings in an arc
across a gentle gap towards High Street.
When it reaches a ruined drystone wall,
either continue along the path, or follow
the course of the wall to the summit trig
point on High Street at 2,718 feet (828
metres). Although views are remarkably
extensive, the broad expanse of grass and
sedge tend to make everything look rather
distant. If time can be spared, then scout
around the edges to peer down ino
deeply-cut dales. Both the path and
the wall run down to a gap at the
Straits of Riggindale.

Loadpot Hill

5. If time is pressing and an early
descent is needed, then branch
left and follow a path down to
Patterdale by way of Angle Tarn,
as described in Walk 2. To continue along the course of the
old Roman road, branch right
and climb uphill a
short way. Watch
out for a path
leading left well
before the blunt
peak of Kidsty
Pike. The aim is
to keep to the
high crest and
cross Rampsgill
Head, then
c o n t i n u e

High Raise

(High Street

Thornthwaite Crag

START

16

across a gentle gap and walk up onto the stony top of High Raise. The summit cairn is just to the right of the path and stands at an altitude of 2,634 feet (802 metres).

6. Follow the path gently downhill to reach a stile at a corner where a fence meets a tall drystone wall. Cross the stile to follow a clear path along the moorland crest, crossing the gentle bump of Raven Howe, then go through a small gate and cross the bump of Red Crag. Don't be tempted too far downhill alongside the fence, but head off to the right and go through a gap in the wall. A gentle climb leads across the broad moorland top of Wether Hill.

7. Follow the path across another broad moorland gap and up onto the slopes of Loadpot Hill. Close to the top is a heap of stonework on a concrete base. This is the ruin of an old shooting hut called Lowther House. The path leads easily to a trig point on top of Loadpot Hill at 2,201 feet (671 metres). While the panorama includes plenty of Lakeland fells, the eye is also drawn across the Vale of Eden to the brooding form of Cross Fell and the bleak moors of the North Pennines.

8. The path continues roughly northwards to leave Loadpot Hill, and looking ahead there aren't really any distinctive hills in sight, only an extensive, rolling moorland slope. Keep an eye on the path, and avoid being drawn off-course to Arthur's Pike, by keeping right at a junction.

9. The path runs roughly north-east and gradually downhill across Whitestone Moor, passing a few areas of heather on the lower slopes. Remain on the clearest path and turn right again at a junction to reach an ancient stone circle called The Cockpit. Bracken grows in patches across the moorlands. Turn left here and follow a path across a gentle gap before rising to a signpost.

10. The old Roman road is signposted ahead and back, but to end this walk you turn left and follow a broad, clear, stony track down across the brackeny slopes of Heughscar Hill. Go through a gate at the bottom to join a road at Roehead.

11. Follow the road downhill and go straight through a

crossroads. Turn left at the next road junction, beside a church, to walk into the village of Pooley Bridge. There are places offering food and drink, as well as a small Tourist Information Centre. Buses depart for Patterdale and Penrith. During the summer there's a service beyond Patterdale, crossing the Kirkstone Pass to descend to Windermere and Bowness.

Kirkstone Pass

The Kirkstone Pass is the highest motor road pass in the Lake District at around 1,500 feet (455 metres). It supposedly takes its name from one of the big boulders on the fellside that is shaped like a little church from a certain vantage point. The Kirkstone Pass Inn, built in 1498, continues to offer food, drink and accommodation to passing travellers. As a high road, it is the first to be blocked by snow each winter, and local people await news of its closure to be sure that winter has finally arrived!

High Street Roman Road

The Romans seem to have been well ensconced in the Vale of Eden before setting their sights on the Lake District. The High Street Roman road appears to have been based on an existing ridgeway track over the fells. The Romans are unlikely to have engineered the route to any degree, but simply incorporated it into their existing network. The old road left Brougham Castle near Penrith, where there was a fort, and climbed along the length of the High Street range before descending to Troutbeck. It must have continued round to the head of Windermere, where there is a Roman fort at Galava. The road was largely contained in the dales, but traces of the route exist on Wrynose and Hardknott Pass, while at the latter there is another fine fort. After descending through Eskdale the road terminated at a fort on the Ravenglass estuary.

4
Ambleside - Dove Crag - Patterdale

Many walkers leave Ambleside with their sights fixed on a circuit of the Fairfield Horseshoe. This walk goes halfway round the horseshoe, climbing Low Pike, High Pike, Dove Crag and Hart Crag. At that point there's a fine view down towards Patterdale and it seems a shame not to go down there. A pleasant ridge route is available in the shape of Hartsop Above How, leading down to the Patterdale road. In summer there are buses back over the top of the Kirkstone Pass to reach Windermere and a linking service back to Ambleside. At other times of the year it's necessary to travel to Penrith and Keswick to return to Ambleside the long way round the fells.

Total distance: 8½ miles (14 kilometres)
Height gain: 2,890 feet (880 metres)
Start: Ambleside: GR376046
Finish: Patterdale: GR395159

1. Find the celebrated Bridge House in Ambleside and then walk up the nearby Kirkstone road. Turn left almost immediately to walk along the narrow Nook Lane. This passes above St. Martin's College and goes through a farmyard at Nook End Farm.

2. Cross Low Sweden Bridge over the tumbling Scandale Beck, then follow a clear track that winds uphill. Go through gate-holes in walls, then follow a drystone wall along the ridge rising to the left. The fellside is covered in bracken. Pass a small stand of pines and scramble up a rock-step. Alternatively, outflank the rock step, then continue to follow the course of the wall along the ridge. The little bump of Low Pike is crossed at 1,657 feet (507 metres).

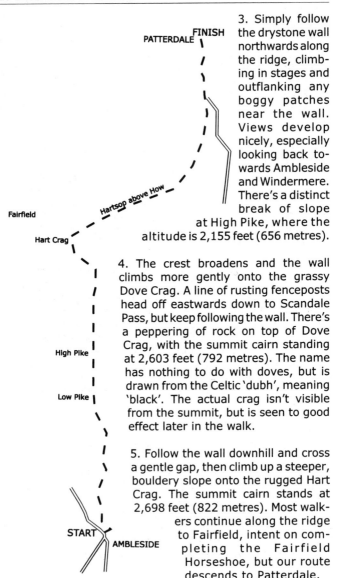

PATTERDALE **FINISH**

Fairfield

Hartsop above How

Hart Crag

High Pike

Low Pike

START

AMBLESIDE

3. Simply follow the drystone wall northwards along the ridge, climbing in stages and outflanking any boggy patches near the wall. Views develop nicely, especially looking back towards Ambleside and Windermere. There's a distinct break of slope at High Pike, where the altitude is 2,155 feet (656 metres).

4. The crest broadens and the wall climbs more gently onto the grassy Dove Crag. A line of rusting fenceposts head off eastwards down to Scandale Pass, but keep following the wall. There's a peppering of rock on top of Dove Crag, with the summit cairn standing at 2,603 feet (792 metres). The name has nothing to do with doves, but is drawn from the Celtic 'dubh', meaning 'black'. The actual crag isn't visible from the summit, but is seen to good effect later in the walk.

5. Follow the wall downhill and cross a gentle gap, then climb up a steeper, bouldery slope onto the rugged Hart Crag. The summit cairn stands at 2,698 feet (822 metres). Most walkers continue along the ridge to Fairfield, intent on completing the Fairfield Horseshoe, but our route descends to Patterdale.

6. A patchy path heads roughly north-east down from the summit of Hart Crag, swinging a little to the east and then winding downhill as it gets clearer. A broad and hummocky crest leads down to a broad and grassy gap, with Hartsop Above How seen ahead. Take in the view to the right, where the slightly overhanging dark face of Dove Crag is seen at the head of Dovedale, along with several rounded fells rising above Hartsop.

7. The path climbs gently from the gap and proceeds along the hummocky crest of Hartsop Above How. The summit rises to 1,870 feet (586 metres) and offers a particularly good view back to the rugged faces of Hart Crag and Fairfield. These are largely unseen by walkers on the Fairfield Horseshoe. The High Street range fills the far horizon, though there's a peep along Ullswater at a lower level. St. Sunday Crag largely obscures the nearby Helvellyn range.

8. Walk down along the crest of Hartsop Above How, reaching a point where there's a rugged break of slope and things are a bit rocky underfoot. There's a ladder stile over a wall to the right, but don't cross it. Follow the wall gently downhill along the ridge and cross another ladder stile over an adjoining wall. The wall offers a sure guide down to Deepdale Park, where there are pleasant and varied clumps of trees. When a fence is reached, cross it using a stile and continue down through denser woodlands. Watch for a path junction and turn left, emerging from the woods to walk down through a field to reach the road.

9. There's a bus stop and phone box at a lay-by on the A592 road. Buses only pass here in summer, linking Glenridding and Patterdale with Windermere and Bowness. During the rest of the year, it's necessary to turn left and follow the road to Patterdale to catch a bus. Walk on the verge or path beside the road, leaving Deepdale and later passing Patterdale Youth Hostel. Patterdale village features the White Lion, Post Office and Patterdale Hotel, then there are bus stops either side of the road, with a year-round service to Penrith. It's possible to get connections via Keswick to return to Ambleside.

5
Rydal - Fairfield - Patterdale

The Fairfield Horseshoe is one of the classic Lakeland circuits, but it's just as much fun to continue over the top of Fairfield and down to Patterdale. This walk offers the chance to appreciate both sides of Fairfield; its relatively smooth southern slopes and its dark, frowning, northern cliff face. The ridge route used for the approach is quite rounded, but the one used for the descent is quite narrow at first, with a distinctly rocky top at Cofa Pike. The broad crest of St. Sunday Crag is crossed before a descent in stages to Patterdale. In summer there are buses back over the Kirkstone Pass, while for the rest of the year it's possible to link buses in a long circuit around the Helvellyn range.

Total distance: 8½ miles (14 kilometres)
Height gain: 3,725 feet (1,135 metres)
Start: Rydal village: GR365062
Finish: Patterdale: GR395159

1. There are regular buses between Ambleside and Grasmere that pass the tiny village of Rydal. It's well worth exploring Dora's Field alongside the church, as well as Rydal Mount, which was Wordsworth's home from 1813 to 1850. Rydal Hall is situated in well-wooded grounds and features a Ramblers' Tea Shop. Walk straight up the steep road through Rydal, past Rydal Mount, to a farm at the top of the road. Turn left to follow a footpath uphill from a gate.

2. The path climbs up a strip of ground between drystone walls at first and there's a ladder stile to cross. Zig-zag more steeply uphill and note that there are some striking views over Rydal Water if you detour to the left from time to time as height is gained. Cross another ladder stile over a wall near the top of Nab Scar, around 1,450 feet (450 metres).

3. The path climbs roughly northwards up a hummocky crest

PATTERDALE **FINISH**

St Sunday Crag

Cofa Pike

FAIRFIELD

Great Rigg

Heron Pike

RYDAL

START

Rydal Water

to reach the top of Heron Pike at 2,003 feet (612 metres). Half the day's ascent is over at this point and the path proceeds in easy ups and downs further along the crest. Another uphill stretch leads to the top of Great Rigg, where there's a cairn at 2,513 feet (767 metres). Views are developing nicely, with Fairfield seen straight ahead.

4. Walk downhill a short way and cross a gentle gap, then climb uphill and note how the gradient eases on the final approach to Fairfield's stony plateau. In mist, this can be a confusing place, with no clear paths and a rash of cairns. The biggest cairn stands on the summit, at 2,863 feet (873 metres). Although views are extensive, it's worth wandering around the plateau edges to appreciate the drops into the dales. In winter the northern edge can be dangerously corniced.

5. Take care leaving the summit of Fairfield. Walk a short way north-east to locate a path that swings north-west down a rocky slope. The prominent little rock peak of Cofa Pike confirms that you're on course. You can climb to the topmost block, or simply scramble past it, then continue down the rugged ridge to reach a narrow gap. The path maintains its north-eastward course and climbs to the stone-strewn top of St. Sunday Crag. There's a cairn at 2,756 feet (841 metres).

Views are largely restricted to the Helvellyn and High Street ranges.

6. Continue along the crest of the fell to start the descent, pausing at a cairn to enjoy a rather fine view of the head of Ullswater. The path descends more steeply to reach a gap. At that point there's a fork to the left leading across the fellside and down to the road in Grisedale. Walkers who want to stay on the fells for a little longer simply stay on the hummocky crest of Birks instead. There's a little pile of stones at 2,040 feet (622 metres).

7. Head roughly eastwards to descend from Birks, following the line of a ruined wall down to a gap at Trough Head. A more substantial drystone wall is found here, surrounding Glemara Park. Follow the wall as it rises and falls gently on the slopes of Arnison Crag. A short detour can include the summit of the crag at 1,424 feet (434 metres) though the view is not particularly extensive at this level.

8. The easiest descent is to follow a path alongside the wall, heading roughly northwards, then turn right along a path to descend to Patterdale village. There's a fork in the path, and keeping to the right leads to the Post Office and White Lion, while keeping left leads to the Patterdale Hotel and bus stops.
9. Buses run along the length of Ullswater to reach Penrith, but it's a long way round the fells, involving a couple of connecting services, if you wish to return to Rydal. In summer bus services run over the Kirkstone Pass to Windermere, where a connecting bus leads more quickly back to Rydal if required.

6
Grasmere - Helvellyn - Glenridding

Many walkers climb Helvellyn from Glenridding or Patterdale, and many more climb it from points on the road north from Grasmere, such as Wythburn, Swirls or Stanah. Almost all of them return to their starting point. This walk is different, making the most of the ascent of Helvellyn by starting from Grasmere, then heading down to Glenridding afterwards. The high-level walk along the crest of the range can be coupled with a descent by way of either Striding Edge or Swirral Edge. Both Grasmere and Glenridding have year-round bus services, while in summer there are also buses between Bowness and Glenridding.

Total distance: 10 miles (16 kilometres)
Height gain: 3,280 feet (1,000 metres)
Start: Travellers Rest, near Grasmere:
GR336089
Finish: Glenridding: GR387168

1. Start at the Travellers Rest on the main road north from Grasmere. There's a bus stop nearby, but if ever you need to park a car here, you have to buy a parking ticket that can later be redeemed for refreshments at the bar. Walk up the road a short way to Mill Bridge and turn right as signposted for Patterdale.

2. A track rises past a few buildings and continues uphill from a gate. You might notice the point at which an underground pipeline, carrying water from Thirlmere to Manchester, is crossed by the track. Climb further uphill and go through another gate, then ford a beck to reach an open slope.

3. You can go either left or right. To the left is a bridleway climbing up beside Little Tongue Gill, while to the right is a

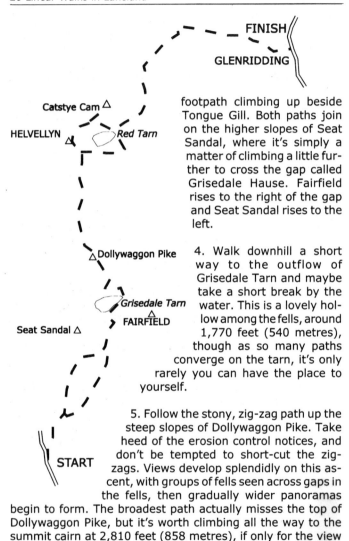

Catstye Cam △

HELVELLYN △   Red Tarn

△ Dollywaggon Pike

Grisedale Tarn
△
FAIRFIELD

Seat Sandal △

START

footpath climbing up beside Tongue Gill. Both paths join on the higher slopes of Seat Sandal, where it's simply a matter of climbing a little further to cross the gap called Grisedale Hause. Fairfield rises to the right of the gap and Seat Sandal rises to the left.

4. Walk downhill a short way to the outflow of Grisedale Tarn and maybe take a short break by the water. This is a lovely hollow among the fells, around 1,770 feet (540 metres), though as so many paths converge on the tarn, it's only rarely you can have the place to yourself.

5. Follow the stony, zig-zag path up the steep slopes of Dollywaggon Pike. Take heed of the erosion control notices, and don't be tempted to short-cut the zig-zags. Views develop splendidly on this ascent, with groups of fells seen across gaps in the fells, then gradually wider panoramas begin to form. The broadest path actually misses the top of Dollywaggon Pike, but it's worth climbing all the way to the summit cairn at 2,810 feet (858 metres), if only for the view down the other side. There's a big difference between the smooth western slopes of the Helvellyn Range and the rough and rocky eastern slopes.

6. To enjoy the Helvellyn range to the full, walk along the high crest rather than along the broad path used by most walkers. Dollywaggon Pike is followed by the broad and stony summit of Nethermost Pike at 2,920 feet (891 metres). After crossing a gap a final pull leads up the stony slopes of Helvellyn. A cross-shelter is passed on the way to the trig point, which is perched close to an edge at 3,118 feet (950 metres). There's a wonderful view down on Red Tarn, which is flanked by the rocky ridges of Striding Edge and Swirral Edge. On a clear day, views can stretch beyond the Lakeland fells to distant Snowdonia and the Cheviot Hills, so it's possible to see England, Wales and Scotland at a glance.

7. You could descend by either Striding Edge or Swirral Edge, but be warned that the edges can be dangerously corniced in the winter, in which case a descent north-west to The Swirls would be safer. Striding Edge involves some hands-on scrambling and features a few exposed stretches along the ridge. Swirral Edge is steep and rocky in places, and while it could be considered as an easier route, it still needs care. The descent via Swirral Edge leads more directly to the outflow of Red Tarn, and there's always the option of including an ascent of the striking pyramidal peak of Catstycam on the way.

8. A clear path proceeds down the valley from Red Tarn, often moving some distance away from Red Tarn Beck. Further downhill, the path crosses the beck using a footbridge. Continue walking downstream alongside Glenridding Beck for a while, then there's a small, metal footbridge off to the left.

9. Cross the footbridge and pass above a rocky gorge where water is drawn off near a small waterfall. Signs warn that you are walking through the Greenside Mine, and there's a request for walkers to stick to the paths and avoid mine workings. Lead was wrested from the mines, which closed in the 1950s.

10. A track leads past a series of former mine buildings, which have mostly been converted into accommodation, including the Swirral Bothy and Glenridding Youth Hostel. The track runs down the valley as parallel strips of concrete, then becomes a broad and stony track as it passes terraced houses further down, on the lower slopes of Sheffield Pike.

11. When the road suddenly bends to the right and drops more steeply, there's a track on the left signposted for Glenridding. Take either the track or the road, as the walk is quickly drawing to a close. The road soon passes the Travellers Rest pub as it enters the village. You started at a pub with that name, and more or less finish at a pub with the same name! A short walk down the road leads to other places offering food and drink, as well as toilets and a Tourist Information Centre. The bus stops are on the main road by the bridge.

Helvellyn

Everyone has heard of Helvellyn, it is one of the most popular fells in the Lake District. Summer and winter, all day and sometimes at night too, you can expect to find several people wandering around the broad summit. It wasn't always like that. In April of 1805 a Manchester walker called Charles Gough fell to his death on Helvellyn and his body wasn't discovered for three months. By that time only his bones remained, with his Irish terrier, Foxey, waiting pitifully alongside. Wordsworth was moved to pen a few lines headed: 'The unfortunate tourist of Helvellyn & his faithful dog'. A memorial, rather worn with the passage of time, tells the story on the brow above Striding Edge. Another rusting memorial along Striding Edge is dedicated to Robert Dixon, who fell while following the Patterdale Foxhounds in 1858. At least this time there were other people around to witness his demise, and apparently, immediately after his fall, he rose to indicate which way the fox had gone, then promptly collapsed and died! A memorial near the top of Helvellyn commemorates the landing of an aeroplane, an Avro piloted by Bert Hinkler and John Leeming, just before Christmas 1926. There was only one man on the summit to witness the landing, and he was pressed into providing a signed statement before the plane took off and returned to Woodford.

7
Aira Force - Old Coach Road - Keswick

The thought of walking from Aira Force to Keswick may leave some walkers shaking their heads in disbelief, but there's actually a good track most of the way, and interesting little paths fill the gaps. There are regular bus services at both ends of the route, with connections via Penrith if a return is needed, though in summer a single bus service links both ends of the walk. Although the summer bus service passes through Dockray, offering the chance to shorten the walk, it would be a pity to miss the charming Aira Force at the start of the day. Buses can be caught around Castlerigg in the summer, saving a road-walk down into Keswick at the end of the day.

Total distance: 12½ miles (20 kilometres)
Height gain: 1,805 feet (550 metres)
Start: Aira Force, near Ullswater: GR401199
Finish: In the middle of Keswick: GR265235

1. Leave the bus at the junction of the main A592 road alongside Ullswater and the A5091 for Dockray. There's immediate access from this junction to a National Trust car park, tea room and toilets. A path goes through a stone gateway to leave the car park, and there are information boards and maps of the paths around Aira Force. Go through two gates and enter a woodland, then go down steps to reach a footbridge over Aira Beck.

2. Cross the footbridge and climb up another flight of steps, then bear left to follow the path across a well-wooded slope. Go down and cross a stone-arched footbridge that offers a fine view of the slender Aira Force plunging into a rocky gorge. A zig-zag flight of steps leads uphill and a right turn leads to a

29

higher stone-arched footbridge, now allowing a view down onto Aira Force.

3. Cross the bridge and continue walking upstream along a path. There are a handful of smaller falls, but nothing as dramatic as the main waterfall. The path pulls away from High Force and goes through a little gate marked for Dockray. Walk through a patch of woodland, then go through another gate and keep walking along a field path. At the next gate, small blue signs point the way to Dockray. Turn left as signposted up a track from a lovely cottage. The little village is quickly reached and there's a pub called the Royal Hotel.

4. In summer the walk could be started from Dockray, as there's a bus service through the village linking Keswick and Patterdale. Follow the minor road signposted for High Row and Dowthwaite Head. The moorland slopes of The Dodds rise ahead and there may be a glimpse of Ullswater below. A road junction and small parking space are reached at Cockley Moor at the corner of a forest.

5. A gate beside the forest is marked with a National Trust sign for Matterdale Common. Go through the gate and follow a clear and obvious stony track alongside the forest. Continue beyond the forest to cross Groove Beck, either using the paved ford or a small footbridge alongside.

6. There's no problem with route-finding on this walk, as the Old Coach Road is such a clear track. When the accompanying fence ends, the track runs free across the moorland slopes of Matterdale Common. There is plenty of boggy ground, spiked with rushes, on either side around Wolfcrag Moss, then the track crosses Mariel Bridge over Mosedale Beck.

7. There's a gradual ascent as the Old Coach Road rises across

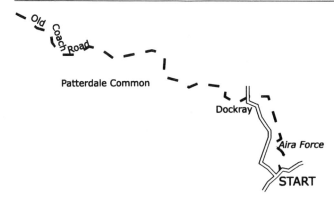

the foot of Clough Head, almost reaching 1,475 feet (450 metres). The ridges and gullies of Blencathra are well displayed to the north and look particularly impressive when the light cuts across them, accentuating their relief. As the track begins to descend, rather more steeply than on the ascent, there are views ahead to Skiddaw, High Seat and High Rigg.

8. As the gradient begins to ease above the old quarries at the Threlkeld Mining Museum, an area of rumpled fellside is all that remains of a Prehistoric settlement. Although there are other tracks criss-crossing the fellside, always walk downhill along the steepest one. Turn left when walls and fences are reached, passing above the farm of Hill Top, then drop down onto the B5322 road in the verdant St. John's in the Vale.

9. Turn right along the road, then quickly left down a minor road to cross St. John's Beck. When the road bends to the right, continue straight up another narrow road to reach St. John's Church, which sits on a pleasant gap between High Rigg and Low Rigg.

10. Turn right at the church and follow a path up onto Low Rigg. The low fell is enclosed, but there are waymark arrows and stiles, indicating the path down past Tewet Tarn to reach a road. Turn left and follow the road down to a junction, then turn left and left again to cross the old Naddle Bridge. A path signposted on the left climbs to Goosewell Farm, where a left

turn up the road leads quickly to Castlerigg Stone Circle. Marvel at this site for a while.

11. In the summer there are occasional buses between Castlerigg Stone Circle and Keswick, or even back to Dockray, Aira Force, Glenridding and Patterdale. Walking down the road into Keswick is easy enough, and the flow of traffic leads into town along the main A591 road. Watch for the road crossing an old railway trackbed, which offers a more pleasant walk into town, crossing the River Greta to reach the old railway station at the Keswick Pool. Follow Station Road into town to finish, and continue through the town centre to reach the bus station if required.

The Old Coach Road

'During our long moorland trudge, the sharp ridges of Saddleback and the distant prospect over the Eden valley have been redeeming features in what must otherwise be described as one of the dullest walks in the district. Nor has the monotony been greatly relieved by our having as a constant vis-à-vis the round Mell Fell.' So wrote the redoubtable M. J. B. Baddeley in an early guide to the Lake District. It just goes to show how wrong some people can be. The Old Coach Road has been incorporated into the C2C Cycleway, which runs from coast to coast across northern England from Whitehaven to Sunderland.

8
Mosedale - Skiddaw House - Bassenthwaite

The Back o' Skidda' might as well be the back of beyond for all that most walkers know of it. While Skiddaw and Blencathra are popular fells, and many people are happy to follow the course of the Cumbria Way between them to reach Caldbeck, rather fewer walkers have experienced the solitude of these rolling moorlands. It's possible to wander at will over the high ground, but it's also worth trekking through the valleys and enjoying a low-level route. Walk from Mosedale to Bassenthwaite via Skiddaw House, linking with the Caldbeck Rambler buses that encircle the fells. These run on Saturdays all year and daily during summer.

Total distance: 10½ miles (17 kilometres)
Height gain: 1,000 feet (300 metres)
Start: Mosedale village: GR230322
Finish: Bassenthwaite village: GR249323

1. Start at the little village of Mosedale, crouched at the foot of the rugged Carrock Fell. There's a signpost pointing along a narrow road for Swinside. Just to the left of the road is an old Friends Meeting House that doubles as a coffee shop. The narrow road leads into a valley also called Mosedale. The village is quickly left behind and the road passes lush green pastures with only a few farm buildings along the way. The higher parts of the dale take on a bleak, boggy, barren aspect that characterises moorlands at the Back o' Skidda'.

2. The road ends at a series of old mines, where geologists enjoy picking around the old spoil heaps. Turn left and cross a little bridge over Grainsgill Beck, and continue walking along a stretch of the Cumbria Way roughly parallel to the River Caldew. This is a clear track, leading past an old,

FINISH

BASSENTHWAITE

Dash Beck

Whitewater Dash

stone, tin-roofed ruin.
The path begins to pull
away from the river, bend-
ing into a side valley drained
by Wiley Gill, where a footbridge is crossed.

3. Keep following the path and rising   *Skiddaw House*
gradually around the lower moorland
slopes of Great Calva. Watch out for a spur to the left, where
the path crosses the higher reaches of the River Caldew, now
no more than a beck. Climb straight towards Skiddaw House
and its sheltering stand of woodland. In the summer months
the heather on the surrounding moorland is flushed purple and
enlivens the otherwise muted colours of the landscape.

4. Skiddaw House was formerly a shepherd's habitation,
whose last occupant, Pearson Dalton, used to walk over the
hills to and from Fell Side. After a period lying empty, the
building was converted into a Youth Hostel. The only access is
on foot, so you'll never find the place surrounded by cars!
You've already walked one of the approaches to Skiddaw
House, and you'll leave on another.

5. Turn right to follow the clearest track away from Skiddaw
House, descending gently and crossing the infant River Caldew
again, then rising to cross the broad Candleseaves Bog. The
track descends gently and suddenly makes a zig-zag to cross
Dash Beck. At this point it's worth scouting around for a good
viewpoint, as Dash Falls lie in a rocky gorge. The full name for
the waterfall is Whitewater Dash. If you're pining to climb a fell
at this point, then you could switch to Walk 9 and climb
Skiddaw, then descend to Keswick.

6. The track is clear and obvious as it proceeds downhill from
the falls, in the shadow of Dead Crags. The slopes on the left
seem to rise higher and higher towards Skiddaw. Continue

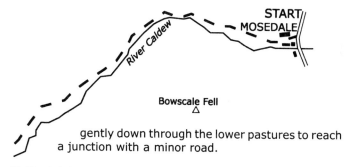

gently down through the lower pastures to reach a junction with a minor road.

7. Straight across the road is the access road for Peter House Farm, and a public bridleway for Bassenthwaite heads off to the left, away from the farm road. Follow the course of the bridleway faithfully through down through the fields to reach the village. There's a pleasant little green in the middle and the Sun Inn offers refreshments, although it isn't immediately apparent, being tucked out of sight.

8. The Caldbeck Rambler bus passes through the village, though it's also possible to walk a short way down School Lane to Chapel, where Bassenthwaite Parish Church is located, to connect with other bus services running from Workington to Keswick and on to Penrith.

Caldbeck Fells

There's a saying that states 'Caldbeck Fells are worth all England else', and if this refers to the mineral wealth underground, then it may well be true. Owing to a complex intrusion of both granite and gabbro in these fells, a bewildering variety of minerals have been formed. Some of the contain uncommon metals, such as tungsten, while others are simply unusual compounds, but with no commercial use. Although mining has ceased, geologists continue to pick through the spoil heaps for specimens, and as some of the minerals fluoresce under ultra-violet light, some collectors will work at night with hand-held UV lamps!

9
Caldbeck - Skiddaw - Keswick

The Cumbria Way passes through the Northern Fells and links Keswick with Caldbeck. For much of the time it stays low in the valleys, though there is a climb over the top of High Pike. Walkers who want to explore the area can stay high for much longer, and this walk from Fell Side to Keswick takes in a series of heights, culminating in the lofty Skiddaw.
The Caldbeck Rambler bus naturally serves Caldbeck, running on Saturdays throughout the year and daily through summer. If you are based at Keswick, then you can walk back to town from Caldbeck and complete this long walk at your leisure, with no need to travel further after reaching town.

Total distance: 18½ miles (30 kilometres)
Height gain: 3,935 feet (1,200 metres)
Start: Caldbeck: GR324398
Finish: In the middle of Keswick: GR265235

1. Make sure you have plenty to eat and drink before leaving Caldbeck, as there's a long moorland march ahead. The route leaves Caldbeck by following the B5299 road, from a clogmaker's warehouse, in the direction of Uldale. Branch left almost immediately along a parallel road for a short way, then go through a small gate to follow a path flanked by hedges. This path leads up to a track junction at Upton. Turn right, then left and follow a narrow old road uphill, marked as 'except for access', and flanked by tall hedges. Go straight through a crossroads and follow a road signposted for Nether Row.

2. Keep climbing along a track to leave the buildings at Nether Row, then at a junction branch left to climb further past old mines. Make a beeline straight uphill for the top of High Pike, regardless of other tracks and paths crossing the slope. The summit is reached at an altitude of 2,157 feet (658 metres).

CALDBECK **START**

High Pike △

Knott △

Whitewater Dash

△ Great Calva

△ SKIDDAW

△ Lonscale Fell

Latrigg △

KESWICK

FINISH

There's a large cairn, a trig point and a stone memorial bench. The view ahead to the Back o' Skidda' is desolate, and only a few fells are seen further into the Lake District. Looking north, however, vast tracts of southern Scotland are seen beyond the plains.

3. Walk roughly southwards from High Pike and turn right along a clear path. This leads across the gentle, heathery bumps of Great Lingy Hill, towards what looks like a garden shed. This wooden hut is left open for the benefit of passing walkers and as it's on a desolate stretch of the Cumbria Way, some stay overnight. Many others use it for a sheltered lunch stop on cold, wet days. There may be a 'bothy book' noting all the comings and goings.

4. Continue along and down the path to reach Grainsgill Beck. If the weather is foul, you can exit downstream easily enough to Mosedale in the hope of catching a bus, otherwise keep walking as follows. Cross over the beck and walk up the rougher, wetter slopes of Miller

37

Moss, gradually swinging to the right across a broad and boggy plateau to reach Knott. A cairn marks the summit at 2,329 feet (710 metres). Views of the rolling moorlands to the Back o' Skidda' seem to become increasingly desolate.

5. Walk roughly south-west down to a gap, following a grassy path that can be vague in places. Veer to the left while crossing a broad gap, in order to avoid boggy patches as much as possible. Climb towards a fence on the crest of the fell ahead, and turn left to follow it to the summit of Great Calva at 2,265 feet (690 metres). There's a curious view southwards, through the valley between Skiddaw and Blencathra, leading the eye to wooded hills beyond Windermere.

6. Double back and follow the line of the fence from Great Calva to the neighbouring moorland rise of Little Calva. It can be particularly wet after a spell of rain. Follow the fence to descend to a zig-zag track at the head of Dash Falls. It's worth making short detours to peer down into a rocky gorge and spot the waterfall, whose full name is Whitewater Dash. If time is running short, then it's possible to follow the track down towards Bassenthwaite and bus services. Refer to Walk 8 for details.

7. There's a steep climb straight ahead, with a wall and fence as guide, to the top of Bakestall. The summit of Bakestall is only a gentle hump, where a pause for breath can be enjoyed. The fence continues uphill and leads most of the way onto Skiddaw. The grass gives way to slaty ground before the summit trig point is reached. This is the highest point on the walk, at 3,054 feet (931 metres) and offers an extensive view. Practically all the prominent Lakeland fells are in view, along with substantial parts of southern Scotland and the North Pennines.

8. The crest of Skiddaw features three broad swellings, then the path heads off to the left for the descent. The summit of Little Man can be crossed by keeping to the right, as the main path simply slices across its northern flanks and doesn't go near the top. The summit rises to 2,837 feet (865 metres) and bears a cairn. If it is visited, then rejoin the main path down below, where it crosses the fence.

9. Walk down the broad and obvious path, where the gentle gradient suddenly gives way to a steeper slope. Grass gives way to heather, then bracken at a lower level, as the path descends alongside Whit Beck. The lower parts of the path are fenced and a right turn towards the bottom leads to a car park at a road-end near the sprawling little fell of Latrigg.

10. Follow the road only a short way, then turn left to walk down a clear path instead. This descends alongside a forest and slices across the steep slopes of Latrigg. It turns around a little valley on the fellside and is known as Spooney Green Lane as it continues downhill. Cross the busy A66 by bridge and turn right at a road junction. A couple of left turns by road, and a bridge over the River Derwent, lead finally into Keswick.

Cumbria Way

Walkers who follow the Cumbria Way generally start in Ulverston and walk northwards through the Lake District to reach Carlisle. The distance is around 70 miles (113 kilometres) and it can be covered comfortable in a week. Many walkers assume that they have to carry all their gear all the way, but this isn't true. The Cumbria Way can be divided into simple one-day walks that tie in well with public transport. Walkers could commute to and from the route by using bus services to Ulverston, Coniston, Elterwater, Great Langdale, Borrowdale and Keswick. Caldbeck can be reached by bus only during the summer, and Carlisle is served all year round. The terminal points of Ulverston and Carlisle are also served by rail.

IO

Buttermere - Dale Head - Keswick

Honister Rambler buses run in circuits between Keswick and Buttermere from April to September each year. If you're relying on buses, then this is essentially a summer walk. Catch the bus to Buttermere, then walk back to Keswick over the high fells at your leisure. Remarkable ridge walking with wonderful views eventually gives way to low-level strolling through woods and fields to return to Keswick. It's possible to finish early and catch the bus on the last leg to Keswick. If the Keswick Launch is running, then there's also the option to sail back across Derwent Water to return to Keswick.

Total distance: 10½ miles (17 kilometres)
Height gain: 3,770 feet (1,150 metres)
Start: Buttermere village: GR175170
Finish: In the middle of Keswick: GR265235

1. The Honister Rambler service consists of two buses running between Keswick and Buttermere; one in a clockwise direction and one anti-clockwise. Choose either one to reach Buttermere village, where the Bridge Hotel, Fish Hotel, Croft House Café and toilets are available. Leave the village on foot and follow the narrow, unfenced road signposted for Keswick above St. James' Church.

2. Head off to the right where there's a small footpath sign and follow a path that climbs more and more steeply up a slope of bracken. A zig-zag stretch climbs steeply, then a gentler stretch runs behind High Snockrigg. There's a level patch of bog at Buttermere Moss, then the path climbs steep and stony to reach the summit cairn on Robinson at 2,417 feet (737 metres). Views develop nicely on this ascent, ending with a fine panorama taking in most of the Lakeland fells.

3. Walk roughly southwards from Robinson's summit and swing left alongside a fence. Cross a gap at Littledale Edge and climb uphill a short way. A path running off to the left leads to the summit of Hindscarth at 2,385 feet (727 metres), or you could simply continue along Hindscarth Edge. If you do go to the summit of Hindscarth, it's worth continuing a short distance beyond to reach a cairn overlooking the Newlands Valley. It's a particularly good viewpoint.

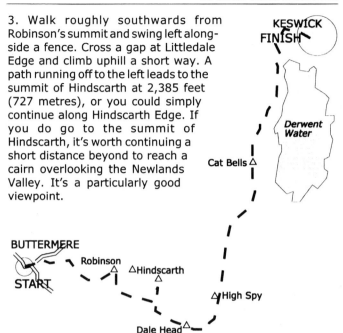

4. The path along Hindscarth Edge gives way to an easy climb onto Dale Head, where a fine summit cairn stands at 2,473 feet (753 metres). Views seem to get better and better on this walk. If you find yourself losing time at this point, there's an easy escape roughly southwards, linking with the course of a fence, leading down to Honister Pass. Honister Rambler buses cross the pass, so it's possible to bail out easily.

5. To continue from Dale Head, follow a path roughly north-east from the summit, swinging right on the way down to land beside the small pool of Dalehead Tarn. Paths converge beyond the tarn, so turn left to walk away from the tarn, then branch right to follow another path uphill onto High Spy. The summit is crowned with a fine pepperpot cairn at 2,143 feet (653 metres). As a viewpoint, it lives up to its name. High Spy with my little eye... most of Lakeland!

41

6. Follow the broad, stony crest onwards. The path is clear and the ridge narrows at the appropriately named Narrow Moor. Continue over the heathery top of Maiden Moor immediately beyond, which rises to 1,887 feet (576 metres).

7. There's a gradual descent to a gap called Hause Gate, which is something of a walkers' crossroads. If time is a problem and you want to intercept a particular bus service on the road below, then exit to the right and hurry down a clear zig-zag path to Manesty.

8. Staying on the tops, however, a short climb along a clear ridge path leads to the final summit of Catbells. Although only 1,481 feet (451 metres) in height, this is a splendid viewpoint, well placed for admiring Borrowdale, Derwent Water, the Vale of Keswick, shapely Skiddaw and the high fells that have been traversed during this day's walk. The ground has been trodden to bare rock by countless thousands of walkers, attesting to its popularity.

9. Continue along the clear ridge path, which descends quite steeply at first. There's a fairly level stretch, then another steep descent towards a road junction. Follow the road down across a cattle grid and into a patch of woodland. People have a nasty habit of parking their cars all over the place hereabouts. It's possible to wait by the cattle grid for a bus back to Keswick, if one is due.

10. To finish the walk using the Keswick Launch, follow a path off to the right to the little launch pier at Hawse End, but try and time your arrival to coincide with a ferry. They run clockwise and anti-clockwise at busy times. Relax and enjoy the lake scenery, then finally follow Lake Road back into Keswick.

11. Die-hard walkers who insist on walking back to Keswick can link paths, tracks and roads by way of Portinscale. It's all well trodden and well signposted. Start by following the path signposted for Hawse End, then turn left and proceed as waymarked and signposted through the woods towards Portinscale. The village is entered by road and there are places offering food and drink.

12. Leave Portinscale and cross a wobbly suspension bridge over the River Derwent. Walk towards the main road, but turn right beforehand to follow a well-trodden field path back into Keswick. Turn right to cross the River Greta using a road bridge and note the Pencil Museum on the left on the way back into town. A right turn leads to the bus station, if you have any further journey to make.

Keswick

The bustling Lakeland town of Keswick is an admirable base for anyone using public transport. There is a range of accommodation options, as well as lots of shops, pubs and restuarants. You could wine and dine at a different place every night for a fortnight. Buses come and go at frequent intervals, running regularly between Workington and Penrith, as well as northwards to Carlisle and southwards to Windermere and Kendal. The Borrowdale Bus runs all through the year, while in summer there are runs over the passes to Buttermere, as well as around the Skiddaw Fells to Caldbeck, and direct services to and from Patterdale. Add to this the ferry services around Derwent Water and you can see that all sorts of walking opportunities are brought within easy reach. The town also boasts some peculiar museums, such as the Pencil Museum and 'Cars of the Stars'. The Theatre by the Lake is another popular attraction.

II

Buttermere – Ennerdale – Wasdale – Seatoller

An entertaining walk can be enjoyed from dale to dale along old packhorse ways in the heart of the Lake District. Starting from Buttermere, this route crosses the Scarth Gap Pass and descends to the Black Sail Hut at the head of Ennerdale. From there it's an easy matter to cross the Black Sail Pass and descend to Wasdale Head. A walk across the Sty Head Pass leads over to Seathwaite and Seatoller at the head of Borrowdale. At that point most walkers would be happy to catch a bus, and there are services along the length of Borrowdale to Keswick, as well as summer services over Honister Pass and back to Buttermere.

Total distance: 14¼ miles (23 kilometres)
Height gain: 3,280 feet (1,000 metres)
Start: Buttermere village: GR175170
Finish: Seatoller, at the head of Borrowdale:
GR245137

1. The Honister Rambler service consists of two buses running between Keswick and Buttermere; one in a clockwise direction and one anti-clockwise. Choose either one to reach Buttermere village, where the Bridge Hotel, Fish Hotel, Croft House Café and toilets are available. Leave the village by walking through the farmyard at Wilkinsyke, then following a clear and obvious path to the lake.

2. The shore of Buttermere is well-wooded, but not so densely that views of the high fells are obscured. At one point a formidable crag juts out into the lake, but there's a path leading straight through a tunnel to pass this obstacle. It was cut on the orders of a previous owner of the big house called

Hassness. There's an open stretch of shore before the path joins the B5289 road.

3. Follow the road beyond the head of the lake, noting how attractive the trees along the shore are. Turn right at Gatesgarth Farm and follow a clear track straight across level fields. It's possible to start the walk at this point as it's on the Honister Rambler bus route, and this move might save up to an hour. Cross the fields and cross Warnscale Beck at the far side, passing through a gate to reach the open fellside.

4. A path slants up to the right, then at a junction on the brackeny fellside, turn left to follow another path up alongside

a small stand of trees. The path climbs and passes through a gate in a fence, then through a gap in a drystone wall, and finally reaches the top of the Scarth Gap Pass around 1,475 feet (450 metres). This is a good leg-up for anyone heading for the higher fells, but on this walk you simply cross over and walk down the other side. The path runs alongside a stand of forest to reach a gate at the bottom. Don't go through the gate, but turn left and follow a track to the Black Sail Hut.

5. The Black Sail Hut Youth Hostel is at the wonderfully wild head of Ennerdale, looking up towards mighty fells such as Pillar and Great Gable. It's very tempting to abandon the walk and book in for the night! Follow the path past the door and down to the River Liza, then cross a footbridge over the flow.

6. Follow a path upstream alongside Sail Beck. It's steep and rugged in places, but it doesn't take too long to reach the top of the Black Sail Pass at 1,778 feet (542 metres). Again, it's a fine springboard for the fells, but for the moment you should simply cross over and walk down the far side. The path zig-zags across Gatherstone Beck and proceeds down through Mosedale, passing through a gate. At the mouth of the dale, turn right down through a gate to the Wasdale Head Inn. If there's time for a drink and a snack, then stop and enjoy a break.

7. Leave the hotel and follow a path straight across the fields to the tiny church of St. Olaf, almost hidden in the trees that fill the graveyard. Have a look inside, then turn left along the track on the far side. Follow the track to the isolated farm at Burnthwaite, then continue along the level, but often stony path beyond. Cross a footbridge over Gable Beck and marvel at the fells towering high all around you.

8. The clearest path rises across the scree slopes of Great Gable, and this path indeed leads directly to the Sty Head Pass. However, watch carefully for a lesser path drifting off to the right, alongside Lingmell Beck. This is the old packhorse way, which many walkers aren't aware of in their haste to follow the other path. The lower route fords the confluence of Piers Gill and Spouthead Gill, then zig-zags up into the rugged dale-head by a most delightful route. Towards the top, head off to

the left to reach the Sty Head Pass around 1,575 feet (480 metres). This popular pass is easily identified even in foul weather and poor visibility as there's a Mountain Rescue stretcher box there.

9. To leave Sty Head, simply follow the gentle path down in the direction of Styhead Tarn. Cross a footbridge over Styhead Gill and continue downstream. The path is bouldery at first, drifting away from the water. A reconstructed stretch zig-zags down a steep and rugged slope to reach Stockley Bridge.

10. Cross Stockley Bridge and admire its graceful arch, then follow a clear path that becomes a good track by the time it reaches the farm buildings at Seathwaite. Food and drink are available at this point in a farmhouse café. If you're in a hurry to catch a particular bus, you could simply follow the road.

11. To continue and avoid the road for a while, turn left through a roofed gap in the buildings. Cross the valley floor and cross a footbridge over the infant River Derwent. Look up the fellside to spot the spoil heaps of old graphite mines that once supplied the pencil industry at Keswick.

12. Turn right to cross Sour Milk Gill and admire the waterfalls, then follow an easy path downstream alongside the River Derwent. The path joins the road and the road leads to a junction with the B5289. Turn left to reach Seatoller, where the bus to Keswick turns around at the entrance to the car park. Food and drink are offered at the Yew Tree Café Bar. Across the road is the Seatoller Barn, which houses old agricultural implements and offers an insight into the history and heritage of Borrowdale.

12

Ravenglass - Irton Road - Miterdale - Boot

The Ravenglass & Eskdale Railway, or t' La'al Ratty, isn't just for the enjoyment of children. It's a proper public transport service for the folk of Eskdale, with miniature steam and diesel engines pulling cute, coloured carriages through the verdant dale. Here's a walk from Ravenglass to Boot, with an option to break the journey at Irton Road. Enjoy the walk over Muncaster Fell and up through Miterdale, then down to Boot, ending with a run along the length of the railway.

Total distance: 12½ miles (20 kilometres)
Height gain: 1,640 feet (500 metres)
Start: Ravenglass Station: GR085965
Finish: Dalegarth Station, near Boot: GR173007

1. Start at Ravenglass Station, either the main line station of the miniature rail terminus alongside. It's worth wandering round the former fishing village before starting the walk. The footbridge crossing the main line, linking the two stations, has a footpath continuing straight to a narrow road. Turn right along this road to reach the Roman fort ruins of Walls Castle.

2. Walls Castle is actually the Bath House of the old fort, as the main structure was sliced through by the railway in 1850. Walk further along the road and turn left at a sign for Newtown Cottage. Another left turn leads along a track that can be muddy in places, especially where it leaves the woods and runs through fields. Rhododendrons grow in profusion in the wood-lands around Muncaster Castle. Watch for a left turn where a track leads out onto the main A595 road at Muncaster Home Farm.

3. Turn right and walk up the road, past the Muncaster Castle

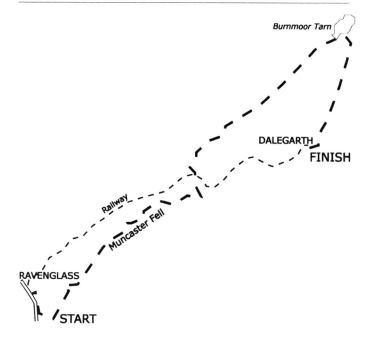

main gate, to reach a prominent road bend. Follow Fell Lane straight uphill from the main road. It's stony and flanked by walls and trees at first, then keep right in a dip to pass Muncaster Tarn. As the track leads into open country it becomes grassy and cuts across the open slopes of Muncaster Fell. The fell isn't too high and the path slices across the slope. You could visit the summit at 758 feet (231 metres) with a short diversion. Views of the higher fells are superb.

4. The path is fairly clear as it leads through bracken and crosses boggy patches. Pass a curious rock slab deeply inscribed with the name 'Ross's Camp 1883'. It's actually an old picnic table. The path is wet and muddy in places and passes down through an old gateway in a wall. There are a few trees on a gap in the fell, notably birch and rowan. Note how well engineered the track is around Silver Knott, before descending into Eskdale. Pass through a gate and watch out for more muddy patches on the way down.

5. When a grassy track is reached on the lower ground, turn left as indicated by a bridleway marker. Pass a house and follow a walled lane to Irton Road Station. Anyone wanting to finish early and spend the rest of the day on the railway can do so at this point. Alternatively, it's possible to start walking at the station and continue as follows.

6. Leave Irton Road Station and turn left along the road, then turn right along a narrow road to enter Miterdale. The road passes a school and continues past an old mill site to enter small stands of forest. Cross the River Mite using either a footbridge or a ford.

7. Rise from the river and turn right to head further into Miterdale, passing Low Place and a few buildings at Miterdale Head. You need to cross the stream on the right and then keep walking upstream. Watch carefully for the line of the path in the lower fields, then continue to the rugged little dale head, where there are charming little crags and waterfalls to admire, with the great dome of Scafell rising beyond.

8. Still keeping to the right, climb up the rugged slope to leave the dale head and cross a broad moorland gap to reach the isolated Burnmoor Lodge. The old lodge is occasionally used by groups and overlooks Burnmoor Tarn, with a view of the high fells around Wasdale and Eskdale.

9. Walk past the building, then bear right and pick up a path heading roughly southwards across a broad and boggy slope. Take care to follow the most well-trodden path, roughly parallel to Whillan Beck, but at some distance from it. The path is later funnelled into lower enclosures and fields.

10. Walk down through the fields and cross a lovely stone bridge beside an old corn mill at Boot. With a careful eye on the train timetable, you'll know if you can take a break at the Burnmoor Inn or the Brook House Inn. To reach the railway terminus, simply turn right along the road after leaving Boot, and Dalegarth Station is located on the right only a short distance away. The railway journey back to Ravenglass is one of the most scenic you could wish to experience.

I3
Boot - Scafells - Glaramara - Seatoller

The Scafell range can be approached from dales as diverse as Eskdale, Wasdale, Borrowdale or Langdale. Of course, whatever way walkers approach the Scafells, they invariably return to their starting point. This walk offers the chance to climb high and stay high on a walk from Eskdale to Borrowdale. The Ravenglass & Eskdale Railway terminates near Boot and after completing the high-level traverse a bus can be caught at Seatoller. If you have to get back to a parked car at Ravenglass, then you'll have to link buses with trains via Keswick, Workington and Whitehaven to return for it, which means a very careful study of timetables. On a walk such as this it's better if you don't have to return for a car.

Total distance: 12½ miles (20 kilometres)
Height gain: 1,640 feet (500 metres)
Start: Dalegarth Station, near Boot: GR173007
Finish: Seatoller, at the head of Borrowdale: GR245137

1. After enjoying a run on the Ravenglass & Eskdale Railway, leave Dalegarth Station and turn left to follow the road towards the head of Eskdale. The little village of Boot is passed, where the Burnmoor Inn is located. Further along the road is the Woolpack Inn, the Youth Hostel and Wha House Farm.

2. Just across the road from Wha House Farm is a parking space, step-stile and public footpath sign at the start of a long ascent leading to Scafell. The path is known as the Terrace Route and it quickly leaves the lower enclosed fields by way of a sheepfold, then follows a drystone wall uphill. Pulling away from the wall and climbing higher, the path crosses a wild

fellside covered in bracken, rock, bog and a few rowan trees. While the path is plain to see, it could easily be lost if you divert from it. Small cairns mark the route over hummocky ground.

3. Cross Catcove Beck and continue climbing fairly gently, but note how the slope steepens on the ascent of Slight Side. There's a rocky little peak here around 2,460 feet (750 metres) and it makes a fine viewpoint as well as an excuse to stop and catch breath. Eskdale looks particularly charming from here.

SEATOLLER **FINISH**

Glaramara △

△ Allen Crags

Great End △   Esk Hause

△ SCAFELL PIKE

SCAFELL △

△ Slight Side

Quagrigg Moss

BOOT START
Dalegarth Station

4. There's a slight dip beyond the summit of Slight Side, then the ascent continues in earnest. A short and relatively easy ascent gives way to a level shoulder at Long Green, which is a good place for admiring the dark, craggy faces of the Scafell range. A final stony slope leads to the top of Scafell, where there's a cairn at 3,162 feet (964 metres). The view is dominated by the proximity of Scafell Pike, but practically all the major Lakeland fells can be seen. The ground quickly gives way to the sea, but even then it's possible to spot the Isle of Man and considerable parts of Southern Scotland on a clear day.

5. There are three main routes between the summits of Scafell and Scafell Pike. The most direct is via Broad Stand but the descent is only really practicable with a rope, as a slip means certain death. Lord's Rake is a rather horribly eroded gash requiring the use of hands as well as feet. The only real option for an ordinary walker is to descend via Foxes Tarn, using a path down a gully full of scree and boulders. The tarn is merely a puddle and below it is a rocky gash that debauches onto a steep and stony slope. Turn left to climb up to the prominent gap called Mickledore, beneath the dark and frowning face of Scafell. Turn right on the gap and climb up a bouldery slope, following a line of cairns, to reach a huge cairn on top of Scafell Pike at 3,210 feet (977 metres). As the highest point in the whole of England, views are naturally extensive and in superb weather can even include glimpses of Scotland, Wales and Northern Ireland.

6. To stay high on the fells and make the most of the day, head north-east to descend from Scafell Pike. A line of cairns marks a path leading down into a rugged gap. Climb uphill and continue to trace the line of cairns across the bouldery slopes of Broad Crag and Ill Crag, crossing a gap between the two rugged tops. Beyond the next gap rises the stony dome of Great End, which could be visited by making a detour, otherwise simply follow the clear path down to the broad gap of Esk Hause. Turn left to drop down to a lower saddle, where there's a drystone cross-shelter where a number of paths converge.

7. If time is pressing and a quick descent is needed from the fells, then a walk down the nearby Ruddy Gill and Grains Gill leads to Stockley Bridge, Seathwaite and Seatoller. The high-level route stays on the tops, first climbing directly uphill from the cross-shelter to the summit of Allen Crags at 2,572 feet (784 metres).

8. There's a gradual descent along the broad and hummocky crest of the fell, passing the little High House Tarn on a gap around 2,130 feet (650 metres). The path becomes a roller-coaster as it traverses a series of humps and bumps, finally reaching the highest point on Glaramara, where there's a cairn at 2,560 feet (780 metres). The view is extensive and

53

enthralling, particularly as the ground falls away so sharply in so many directions. Make the most of it.

9. The descent is roughly northwards and there are a couple of paths heading off in that direction. The one to the left is rough and rocky, while the one to the right actually involves a short scramble. Either way, continue down the broad and hummocky crest towards Thorneythwaite Fell. The path zig-zags more and more to the right until it runs parallel to Comb Gill in a valley.

10. Go through a little gate and continue down a more wooded slope. The path turns left and reaches a junction with the farm access road from Thorneythwaite and the B5289 road in Borrowdale. Simply turn left and cross the River Derwent and walk to the huddle of houses at Seatoller. The bus to Keswick turns around at the entrance to the car park. Food and drink are offered at the Yew Tree Café Bar. Across the road is the Seatoller Barn, which houses old agricultural implements and offers an insight into the history and heritage of Borrowdale.

T' La'al Ratty

In 1871 iron was being mined in Eskdale and loads were taken to Drigg Station by horse and cart. In May 1873 the Ravenglass & Eskdale Railway was incorporated, a standard gauge line was contructed and was operational by May 1875. The line was badly constructed and poorly maintained, then became uneconomic following the closure of the mines, with services running in a haphazard fashion. A narrow gauge railway was constructed between 1915 and 1917, and by 1920 the terminus at Boot was replaced by one at Dalegarth. The line was taken over by the Keswick Granite Company in 1949 to serve a quarry, with the narrow gauge line sandwiched between standard gauge lines. Following another period of closure, the line was bought by the Ravenglass & Eskdale Preservation Society in 1960 and has been developed as both a public transport service and a popular attraction ever since. Ravenglass Station has been converted into a charming railway hostelry called the Ratty Arms.

14
Langdale - Scafell Pike - Seatoller

This walk is a high-level alternative to the walk over the passes between Langdale and Borrowdale. You need to be sure to use the first bus from Ambleside into Great Langdale. You also need to hit a late bus out of Borrowdale, or make sure that you can obtain connections via Keswick if you need to get back to Ambleside after finishing the walk. This route climbs Bowfell and stays high all the way to Scafell Pike, with a descent along the Corridor Route into Borrowdale. Tough fellwalkers could also include an ascent of Great Gable simply by climbing it directly from Styhead Pass.

Total Distance: 12½ miles (20 kilometres)
Height gain: 4,135 feet (1,260 metres)
Start: Old Dungeon Ghyll Hotel, Great Langdale:
GR286061
Finish: Seatoller, at the head of Borrowdale:
GR245137

1. The bus serving Great Langdale turns round near the Old Dungeon Ghyll Hotel. Don't go to the hotel, but continue along the road to a junction, then follow the access road across level fields to Stool End Farm. Go through the farmyard and walk up a track, then turn right and start following a path up the broad ridge above. A small gate gives way to the open fell and there are good views back through Langdale.

2. Follow the path steeply uphill, noticing how it has been reconstructed. The broad ridge is called The Band and the path gradient eases for a while. There's a final steep ascent to a gap in the fells where a few little puddles are known as Three Tarns. In dry weather they can vanish altogether, while in winter they can either be frozen or completely covered with snow.

3. Turn right to follow a steep, rough and stony path up onto

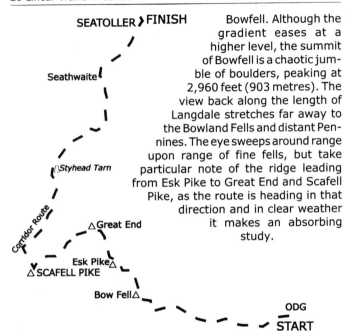

SEATOLLER > FINISH

Seathwaite

Styhead Tarn

Corridor Route

△ Great End

Esk Pike△
△ SCAFELL PIKE

Bow Fell△

ODG
START

Bowfell. Although the gradient eases at a higher level, the summit of Bowfell is a chaotic jumble of boulders, peaking at 2,960 feet (903 metres). The view back along the length of Langdale stretches far away to the Bowland Fells and distant Pennines. The eye sweeps around range upon range of fine fells, but take particular note of the ridge leading from Esk Pike to Great End and Scafell Pike, as the route is heading in that direction and in clear weather it makes an absorbing study.

4. The boulders around the summit of Bowfell give way to a rugged path heading roughly northwards, though veering to the left down to Ore Gap. The gap is reddish underfoot due to exposed haematite iron ore. Climb straight uphill to continue along the ridge, quickly reaching the rocky summit of Esk Pike at 2,903 feet (885 metres). Scafell Pike and neighbouring fells look so much closer.

5. The rugged ridge of Esk Pike leads down to the broad saddle of Esk Hause. If time appears to be running out around this point, then it's a simple matter to drop down to the right and link with the lower line of descent to Borrowdale as described in Walk 15. To climb to Scafell Pike, however, simply cross the broad gap of Esk Hause and follow the cairned path in the direction of Great End.

6. As the path climbs onto the slope of Great End, it also veers to the left, so that it misses the summit completely and climbs over the rugged crest of Ill Crag. There's a little gap to cross, then the path picks its way across the bouldery Broad Crag, narrowly missing the summit. Drop down into a little gap, but one with steep and rocky sides, and climb up onto the broad and bouldery top of Scafell Pike. The huge summit platform cairn stands at 3,210 feet (978 metres).

7. Enjoy the view, which is naturally extensive as this is the highest mountain in England. In clear weather it's possible to identify every notable fell in the Lake District. In really clear weather you could pick out the Pennines, southern Scotland, North Wales and the Isle of Man. Exceptional clarity allows a distant view of features in Northern Ireland. In mist, of course, you'll see nothing at all!

8. Follow a cairned path roughly north-west down a bouldery slope and swing right away from a gap between Scafell Pike and Lingmell. A path crosses the head of an awesome rocky ravine called Piers Gill. Peer into it, but don't even think about descending it. The path known as the Corridor Route cuts across the rugged fellside and offers a line of descent to Borrowdale. Note that there's one point where the path appears to stop at a wall of rock. Scramble over this obstacle to continue along the line of the path. The stony gully of Skew Gill needs to be crossed before a slight climb leads onto Styhead Pass. This popular pass is easily identified even in foul weather and poor visibility as there's a Mountain Rescue stretcher box there.

9. Tough walkers could consider an ascent of Great Gable, but others might be daunted at the size and ruggedness of the fell and be happy to leave it for another day. To leave Sty Head, simply follow the gentle path down in the direction of Styhead Tarn. Cross a footbridge over Styhead Gill and continue downstream. The path is bouldery at first, drifting away from the water. A reconstructed stretch zig-zags down a steep and rugged slope to reach Stockley Bridge.

10. Cross Stockley Bridge and admire its graceful arch, then follow a clear path that becomes a good track by the time it

reaches the farm buildings at Seathwaite. Food and drink are available at this point in a farmhouse café. If you're in a hurry to catch a particular bus, you could simply follow the road.

11. To continue and avoid the road for a while, turn left through a roofed gap in the buildings. Cross the valley floor and cross a footbridge over the infant River Derwent. Look up the fellside to spot the spoil heaps of old graphite mines that once supplied the pencil industry at Keswick.

12. Turn right to cross Sour Milk Gill and admire the waterfalls, then follow an easy path downstream alongside the River Derwent. The path joins the road and the road leads to a junction with the B5289. Turn left to reach Seatoller, where the bus to Keswick turns around at the entrance to the car park. Food and drink are offered at the Yew Tree Café Bar. Across the road is the Seatoller Barn, which houses old agricultural implements and offers an insight into the history and heritage of Borrowdale.

The Corridor Route

Early guides operating from Borrowdale used to take tourists up to Scafell Pike along a route known as the Guide's Route. It's now called the Corridor Route and remains a popular choice among walkers. However, it's an easy matter for keen fellwalkers to climb Scafell Pike by other routes from Borrowdale, or from Langdale, Eskdale or Wasdale. As most who climb Scafell Pike seem to reach the summit around lunchtime, it can appear a very busy place. While some walkers will climb it in any weather, it needs care and the obvious bonus when climbing it on a fine day is the incredibly interesting and extensive view.

15
Langdale - Angle Tarn - Sty Head - Seatoller

A fairly straightforward walk from dale to dale. The celebrated Cumbria Way runs from Great Langdale to Borrowdale, but here's a route that runs a little higher and offers easy access to a couple of fells on the way. The road is based on old packhorse ways that ran from dale to dale, which walkers have gratefully maintained as through routes. Buses run from Ambleside to the Old Dungeon Ghyll Hotel in Great Langdale. Buses from Seatoller run along the length of Borrowdale to Keswick, from where there are services back to Ambleside.

Total Distance: 10 miles (16 kilometres)
Height gain: 2,625 feet (800 metres)
Start: Old Dungeon Ghyll Hotel, Great Langdale: GR286061
Finish: Seatoller, at the head of Borrowdale: GR245137

1. The bus serving Great Langdale turns round near the Old Dungeon Ghyll Hotel. This is a traditional Lakeland hostelry, with toilets alongside, but you'll probably be too early to enjoy a drink. Walk round the back of the hotel and follow a track up through a gate. There's a National Trust sign for Mickleden. Follow the track below Raven Crag, where climbers might be spotted making sport high above you.

2. There's another gate further along the track. The way ahead is stony, but easy to follow. The rocky, domed summit of Pike o' Stickle towers high above. Stone axes were laboriously chipped from a hard band of rock near the summit, then traded as far away as France. All around are hummocky moraines, deposited by the glacier that carved out the great U-shaped valley of Mickleden.

59

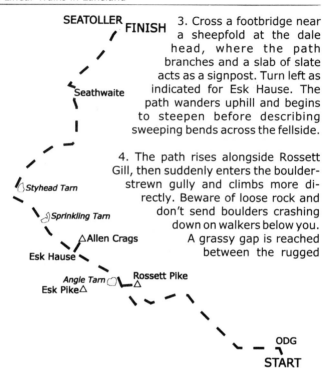

SEATOLLER FINISH

Seathwaite

Styhead Tarn

Sprinkling Tarn

△Allen Crags

Esk Hause

Angle Tarn ◯ Rossett Pike
Esk Pike△ △

ODG
START

3. Cross a footbridge near a sheepfold at the dale head, where the path branches and a slab of slate acts as a signpost. Turn left as indicated for Esk Hause. The path wanders uphill and begins to steepen before describing sweeping bends across the fellside.

4. The path rises alongside Rossett Gill, then suddenly enters the boulder-strewn gully and climbs more directly. Beware of loose rock and don't send boulders crashing down on walkers below you. A grassy gap is reached between the rugged

Bowfell and the gentler Rossett Pike. A right turn and a few minutes' stroll leads to the summit of Rossett Pike at 2,106 feet (642 metres). There's a grand view back along the length of Mickleden and far beyond.

5. Follow the path down to Angle Tarn and cross the outflowing beck. Climb uphill and over a rise at Tongue Head. Another uphill stretch leads to a broad gap where there's a drystone cross-shelter. It's an ideal spot for lunch if there's a chilly breeze. Just above the cross-shelter is the rugged hump of Allen Crags, which can be climbed in a matter of a few minutes. The summit is at 2,572 feet (784 metres) and again there are splendid views. Drop back down to the shelter.

6. Follow the path down from the cross-shelter, in the direction

of Great Gable, passing beneath the dark, craggy, northern face of Great End. There are other paths branching off, but keep to the main one, passing the lovely Sprinkling Tarn on the way down to Sty Head. This popular pass is easily identified even in foul weather and poor visibility as there's a Mountain Rescue stretcher box there.

7. Tough walkers could consider an ascent of Great Gable, but others might be daunted at the size and ruggedness of the fell and be happy to leave it for another day. To leave Sty Head, simply follow the gentle path down in the direction of Styhead Tarn. Cross a footbridge over Styhead Gill and continue downstream. The path is bouldery at first, drifting away from the water. A reconstructed stretch zig-zags down a steep and rugged slope to reach Stockley Bridge.

8. Cross Stockley Bridge and admire its graceful arch, then follow a clear path that becomes a good track by the time it reaches the farm buildings at Seathwaite. Food and drink are available at this point in a farmhouse café. If you're in a hurry to catch a particular bus, you could simply follow the road.

9. To continue and avoid the road for a while, turn left through a roofed gap in the buildings. Cross the valley floor and cross a footbridge over the infant River Derwent. Look up the fellside to spot the spoil heaps of old graphite mines that once supplied the pencil industry at Keswick.

10. Turn right to cross Sour Milk Gill and admire the waterfalls, then follow an easy path downstream alongside the River Derwent. The path joins the road and the road leads to a junction with the B5289. Turn left to reach Seatoller, where the bus to Keswick turns around at the entrance to the car park. Food and drink are offered at the Yew Tree Café Bar. Across the road is the Seatoller Barn, which houses old agricultural implements and offers an insight into the history and heritage of Borrowdale.

16
Langdale - High Raise - Rosthwaite

Most walkers who wander round the Langdale Pikes are completing only a short circular walk from the New Dungeon Ghyll Hotel. After all the effort involved climbing onto the Pikes, it seems a shame to go down so early. This walk climbs Harrison Stickle, then continues over High Raise and ends with a descent to Rosthwaite in Borrowdale. Buses run from Ambleside to the New Dungeon Ghyll Hotel in Great Langdale. Buses from Rosthwaite run along the length of Borrowdale to Keswick, from where there are services back to Ambleside.

Total distance: 8 miles (13 kilometres)
Height gain: 2,475 feet (755 metres)
Start: New Dungeon Ghyll Hotel, Great Langdale: GR295065
Finish: Rosthwaite, in Borrowdale: GR258149

1. The bus serving Great Langdale passes close to the New Dungeon Ghyll Hotel. Walk past the hotel and follow a path between it and the Sticklebarn. Both places offer food and drink, but it may be too early and there's a walk to be done! Turn left at a path junction, away from Mill Gill, then right at a gate to walk up through a small field. The open fellside is reached at a stile alongside a beck called the Dungeon Ghyll, which flows from a pronounced cleft on the slopes of Harrison Stickle.

2. Follow the path uphill, steeply at times, towards Harrison Stickle. Some parts are pitched and other parts cross bare rock, and the chasm of the Dungeon Ghyll is always down to the left. A pleasant, grassy, break of slope is reached, where a small knoll allows a fine view along the length of Great Langdale.

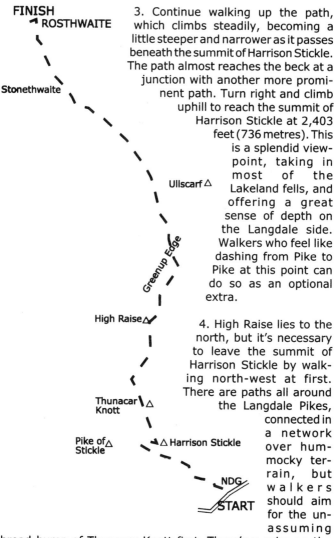

FINISH
ROSTHWAITE

Stonethwaite

Ullscarf △

Greenup Edge

High Raise △

Thunacar
Knott △

Pike of △
Stickle

△ Harrison Stickle

NDG

START

3. Continue walking up the path, which climbs steadily, becoming a little steeper and narrower as it passes beneath the summit of Harrison Stickle. The path almost reaches the beck at a junction with another more prominent path. Turn right and climb uphill to reach the summit of Harrison Stickle at 2,403 feet (736 metres). This is a splendid viewpoint, taking in most of the Lakeland fells, and offering a great sense of depth on the Langdale side. Walkers who feel like dashing from Pike to Pike at this point can do so as an optional extra.

4. High Raise lies to the north, but it's necessary to leave the summit of Harrison Stickle by walking north-west at first. There are paths all around the Langdale Pikes, connected in a network over hummocky terrain, but walkers should aim for the unassuming broad hump of Thunacar Knott first. There's a cairn on the summit at 2,351 feet (723 metres).

5. A vague path runs gently downhill from Thunacar Knott, then is joined by a path from Pavey Ark before crossing a broad, grassy, moorland gap. A gentle climb is accomplished on a clearer path that leads to the summit cairn on High Raise. This is in a rocky area known as High White Stones at 2,500 feet (762 metres). Although this is one of the most central fells in the Lake District, and views are quite extensive, the broad moorland crest makes everything look distant, lacking any real sense of depth.

6. Walk a short way north-east to join a line of rusting fenceposts, which are the remains of an old boundary fence. These can be followed a short way north, then north-east, down the fellside to reach a broad gap at Greenup. This is a notable turning point for walkers, with routes heading straight on for Ullscarf, or right for Easedale and Grasmere, but our descent is left for Borrowdale. You have the option at this point of crossing Ullscarf via Walk 17 to Keswick.

7. Turn left to follow a path across a boggy area to reach Greenup Edge, where the ground begins to fall more prominently. There's a fine view down into Borrowdale from the top of Lining Crag, and a steep path descends alongside the crag on its way into the valley.

8. The path runs alongside Greenup Gill, which is a pleasant watercourse full of small waterfalls and pools. The valley sides are dotted with boulders and covered in grass or bracken. Greenup Gill reaches a confluence with Langstrath Beck at a footbridge. This is a popular place for people to take a summer dip as there's a campsite only a short way downstream.

9. Don't cross the footbridge, but simply continue along the valley path. The path drifts away from the river and becomes quite broad and stony. There are occasional gates to go through and patches of woodland along the way. At one point there's a path on the left offering a link with the little huddled hamlet of Stonethwaite, but to reach Rosthwaite, stay on the main path.

10. After passing below a slope covered in oak trees, the path drifts between fields and passes through another gate on a

bend close to the river. When a fine single-arched stone bridge is reached near Hazel Bank, turn left to cross the river. The B5289 road at Rosthwaite is reached close to the bus stop. If there is any time to spare, then wander round the little village, which is rather quaint. Food and drink are offered at the Borrowdale Hotel, the Royal Oak and the Flock In Café. There's also a small Post Office shop and toilets.

Cumberland Pencils

Strange to think that the humble pencil owes its origins to events around Borrowdale. When graphite was first discovered in the dale, it was simply used in its raw, soft, black form for marking sheep. Later, strips of graphite were enclosed between strips of wood for easier handling, and these implements were further refined to become pencils. The industry became so well established in nearby Keswick that when the graphite was exhausted, other sources were located overseas and imported. Even local wood was abandoned in favour of imported wood, and the development of coloured pencils was an additional spin-off. Anyone with a passion for pencils should make tracks for the Pencil Museum at Keswick, which offers a full and entertaining history of the industry.

17
Grasmere - Ullscarf - Bleaberry Fell - Keswick

Here's a walk that traverses the most central fells in the Lake District. Be warned at the outset that the broad moorlands around Ullscarf and High Seat are quite boggy, though they are more easily passable after a dry or frosty spell. It's possible to walk from Grasmere, up onto Helm Crag, then along a roller-coaster ridge, continuing over Ullscarf, High Seat and Bleaberry Fell, before descending to Walla Crag and Keswick. With an eye on the timetables you can tie in with a bus back to Grasmere.

Total distance: 15½ miles (25 kilometres)
Height gain: 3,380 feet (1,030 metres)
Start: In the middle of Grasmere: GR337076
Finish: In the middle of Keswick: GR265235

1. Start on the little green in the middle of Grasmere and follow Easedale Road gently uphill. Pass the Youth Hostel and a small car park, and maybe make use of a path running parallel to the road to approach Goody Bridge. The road later runs unenclosed through a meadow, then ends suddenly.

2. Follow a track up through a gate, then turn right at a junction as signposted for Helm Crag. A well-constructed path climbs up a wooded slope, then makes sweeping zig-zags up the bracken-clad fellside. When it finally gains the crest of Helm Crag there are fine views back across the Vale of Grasmere. The highest point on Helm Crag is a tilted monolith known as The Howitzer, whose summit can be gained only by hands-on scrambling. It rises over 1,300 feet (395 metres).

3. Follow a steep path a short way down to a little gap, then climb up onto the hummocky crest of Gibson Knott. This can

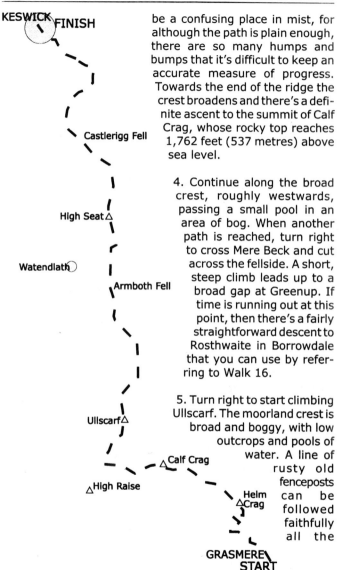

be a confusing place in mist, for although the path is plain enough, there are so many humps and bumps that it's difficult to keep an accurate measure of progress. Towards the end of the ridge the crest broadens and there's a definite ascent to the summit of Calf Crag, whose rocky top reaches 1,762 feet (537 metres) above sea level.

4. Continue along the broad crest, roughly westwards, passing a small pool in an area of bog. When another path is reached, turn right to cross Mere Beck and cut across the fellside. A short, steep climb leads up to a broad gap at Greenup. If time is running out at this point, then there's a fairly straightforward descent to Rosthwaite in Borrowdale that you can use by referring to Walk 16.

5. Turn right to start climbing Ullscarf. The moorland crest is broad and boggy, with low outcrops and pools of water. A line of rusty old fenceposts can be followed faithfully all the

way to the summit, where there's a cairn at 2,370 feet (726 metres). This is one of the most central fells in the Lake District and views are extensive, though the broad moorland shoulders obscure nearby dales.

6. Follow the line of old fenceposts to reach a bit of rock nearby where there's a corner of a post and wire fence. Turn right and follow the fence further downhill. The broad moorland slope is pitched at an easy gradient, but beware the sudden appearance of Standing Crag, and outflank it by following a path to the right. The fence leads across a broad and boggy moorland gap, with a view of Blea Tarn down to the left. There's a gate in the fence where a bridleway runs over from Dob Gill beside Thirlmere to the little farming hamlet of Watendlath.

7. You can use the course of the fence as a sure guide all the way along the broad moorland crest. As it can be seen stretching ahead, occasionally turning a corner, you can either walk right beside it, or simply keep it in view and wander at will through the grass and heather. Just try and avoid the green patches of sphagnum moss and ankle-twisting holes concealed in the heather. The fence rises to a cairn on High Tove at 1,665 feet (515 metres). There's a gate in the fence on High Tove, where a path crosses from Armboth over to Watendlath.

8. Follow the fence ever-northwards along the broad moorland crest, but bear in mind that it runs through some nasty patches of bog around The Pewits that are best given wide berth. Pick the driest line you can find, but keep the line of the fence in view. There's drier footing on the short and easy ascent to the summit of High Seat, where there's a trig point and a cairn on rival bumps, with the fence running between them. The trig point stands at 1,995 feet (608 metres), and views from the summit are extensive and excellent.

9. Continuing northwards, there's an awkward expanse of boggy hollows and heathery hummocks, with a slight ascent onto Bleaberry Fell. The heathery top bears a cairn at 1,932 feet (589 metres). As the ground falls away on most sides, views are quite good, but in some respects they improve once the descent begins.

10. There's a path descending roughly north-west, winding about on the heathery slopes and crossing a shoulder called Brown Knotts, where the gradient eases. Swinging more to the north, this path intersects a well-trodden and popular path leading to Walla Crag. To visit the highest point, at 1,234 feet (376 metres), it's necessary to cross a wall using a stile, where there's a fine view down to Keswick and Derwent Water, stretching up through Borrowdale.

11. Leave Walla Crag by following the path roughly north-east, down alongside the wall, then alongside Brockle Beck, crossing a little footbridge to reach a farm road at Rakefoot. Turn left to walk down the road, but look out for a path on the left leading across another footbridge. Continue downstream along a wooded path, which broadens before you leave the woods near Springs Farm. Continue along the road, which is Springs Road, and turn left at the end to walk straight down into the middle of Keswick.

Grasmere

Walkers might choose to base themselves in Grasmere and avail themselves of good bus links with the rest of the Lake District. Buses run daily through the village, linking with Keswick, Ambleside, Windermere and Kendal. Alternatively, you can walk out of Grasmere, over the fells, and link a series of buses to return to the village. There are two youth hostels, as well as hotels and guest houses, and a splendid choice of places to eat and drink in the evenings. Many of Wordsworth's old homes, as well as the family burial plot, are within easy reach. The village is also famous for its delicious Grasmere Gingerbread, which can be obtained from the little cottage near the church. Just follow your nose and queue alongside the American and Japanese tourists!

18
Langdale - Blea Rigg - Loughrigg - Ambleside

There's a fine walk from Langdale to Ambleside, wandering around along a broad and hummocky crest, taking in Blea Rigg, Silver Howe and lovely Loughrigg Fell. Bus access is easy. Simply use the service from Ambleside to the New Dungeon Ghyll Hotel in Great Langdale, then walk back at your leisure. While it's tempting to climb the Langdale Pikes at an early stage in the walk, try and resist the urge and explore the ins and outs of the broad Blea Rigg instead. Silver Howe and Loughrigg Fell are notable viewpoints, and there's a feeling of being high in the fells even though the route spends much of its time heading downhill.

Total distance: 9½ miles (15 kilometres)
Height gain: 2,950 feet (900 metres)
Start: New Dungeon Ghyll Hotel, Great Langdale: GR295064
Finish: On Kelsick Road in Ambleside: GR376044

1. The bus serving Great Langdale passes the New Dungeon Ghyll Hotel. Just beyond the hotel, to the right of a cottage, a gate gives access to a path. Walk up through a small field, then follow a well-constructed path upstream alongside Mill Gill, also known as Stickle Gill. At a higher level cross over a footbridge.

2. Follow the path further upstream, pausing from time to time to enjoy splendid little waterfalls in the bouldery beck. The path is rather more rugged towards the top, corssing the beck and finally reaching a bouldery dam at Stickle Tarn. Rising above the waters are Harrison Stickle and the awesome cliff

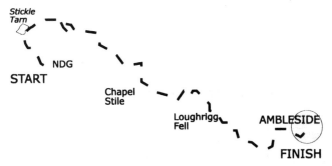

of Pavey Ark. Looking carefully at the cliff, you can distinguish a thin green line rising diagonally from the lower right to the upper left of the crag. Look more carefully and you may spot scramblers picking their way up along the line. It's known as Jack's Rake, and you may be pleased to hear that it forms no part of this walking route!

3. Cross the outflow from Stickle Tarn and follow a path along the shore. Watch carefully for a vague path branching away to the right, while most other walkers will continue towards Pavey Ark. The vague path runs roughly north-east towards Blea Rigg, but it wriggles around on the slope, dodging boggy patches and crossing hummocky ground. The crest will be reached around 1,800 feet (550 metres) and there's a view over to Easedale as well as along Langdale.

4. Turn right to follow the clearest path along the broad and hummocky crest. Although the general trend is downhill, there are lots of little ups and downs along the way, and some of them may be steep and rocky. The path swings to left and right, usually to avoid ascents or boggy hollows. Make the most of the views in clear weather, and keep an eye on your map in poor visibility.

5. Although there are a handful of little pools marked on the map, sitting on the broad crest, the largest of them isn't immediately apparent. It lies in a hollow near Lang Howe and is almost entirely covered in sedge, so it doesn't look like a pool except for a tiny bit of water seen in the middle. Follow the path

71

onwards and climb up onto the prominent little bump of Silver Howe at 1,292 feet (394 metres). There's a particularly fine view over the Vale of Grasmere from here.

6. A path leads down from the summit of Silver Howe and maintains a view over the Vale of Grasmere, passing a large cairn on the way down. Keep walking along the hummocky crest, sometimes with a view over to Elterwater. There are all sorts of other paths around, but keep to the clearest one to drop down onto a prominent little gap.

7. Although paths criss-cross all over the little gap, follow a clear path that accompanies a drystone wall onwards. The wall climbs up a slope of bracken and the path goes through a little gate. The line of the path narrows and passes between stands of trees on the descent to a minor road at Red Bank.

8. Just across the road is a short descent signposted for Loughrigg Terrace. The path quickly passes through a patch of woodland and emerges on an open slope. Loughrigg Terrace is the natural continuation gently downhill, but to stay high you should turn right up a steep zig-zag path. This leads to the summit of Loughrigg Fell where there is a trig point and cairn at 1,101 feet (335 metres). This is perhaps the best viewpoint of the day's walk, seeming to embrace all that's best among the Lakeland fells, despite its relative lack of height.

9. There's a clear path running roughly south-east along the broad and hummocky crest of Loughrigg, mostly in the form of a grassy, green ribbon flanked by bracken. However, there are numerous other paths to left and right that can cause confusion, especially in mist. In fine weather there sould be no problem, but it's a good idea to keep an eye on the map throughout. You should be walking roughly in the direction of Windermere, when you can see it. Enjoy the roller-coaster walk and keep to the high crest all the way down to the little pool called Lily Tarn. It's worth making a short diversion onto Todd Crag at that point, for a splendid view along the length of Windermere.

10. A path can be followed north-east downhill from Lily Tarn, and this is naturally funnelled down a wooded slope towards

a house. Simply walk down the steep and narrow access road to land on a narrow minor road at the bottom. Turn right to follow the road round a bend, then left to cross a fine stone-arched bridge. There's a choice of paths, straight on or to the right. The one leading straight on reaches Ambleside by way of Stoney Lane and the Police Station, close to the celebrated Bridge House. The path to the right runs through Borrans Park and can be used to approach Ambleside by way of the Parish Church, which is perhaps handier for the bus stops on Kelsick Road.

Ambleside

The busy streets of Ambleside contain a bewildering number of outdoor gear shops. If it rains all day, then a tour around them all makes for an interesting expedition. No other town in the world seems to have such a concentration of gear outlets, so if you can't get what you need here, you probably can't get it anywhere! There are also plenty of places to stay, as well as plenty of pubs and restaurants offering food and drink. As a base for walkers it seems to have everything, including good bus connections. Regular runs lead south to Windermere and Kendal, or north to Grasmere and Keswick. There are buses to Hawkshead, Coniston and Great Langdale, as well as quick and easy links with the ferry services on Windermere. In the summer there are buses over Kirkstone Pass to Patterdale, so that all manner of splendid walking routes become possible, allowing you to stride out with confidence along entire ranges of fells, knowing you can get back to base afterwards.

19
Coniston - Coniston Fells - Wrynose - Langdale

The Coniston Fells rise proudly above Coniston village and while most walkers simply climb the Old Man, many others do no more than complete a circular walk over the tops. Using buses it's possible to enjoy more than just the Coniston Fells. First, head for Coniston using services from Ambleside. You can enjoy a fine romp along the main ridge, then continue across the Wrynose Pass and enjoy a walk over Crinkle Crags too. A descent can be made via The Band to the Old Dungeon Ghyll Hotel in time for the last bus back to Ambleside. With careful attention to timetables, this walk can be done using bus services from more distant points such as Windermere or Ulverston.

Total distance: 13 miles (21 kilometres)
Height gain: 4,755 feet (1,450 metres)
Start: At the Black Bull in Coniston: GR302975
Finish: Old Dungeon Ghyll Hotel, Great Langdale: GR286061

1. Coniston is a big village with plenty of shops and pubs if you need food and drink. The Black Bull stands beside a bridge in the middle of Coniston, and the Sun Inn is signposted up a narrow road on the other side of the bridge. Walk up the road to the inn, then turn right as indicated by a footpath sign.

2. A clear path heads for Church Beck and follows it upstream, passing the Miner's Bridge. The path climbs more steeply up a rugged slope and reaches a bend on a track. Stop at this point and take in the view all around the Coppermines Valley, which is full of ruins, shafts and spoil heaps. The solitary whitewashed building in view is the Coppermines Youth Hostel.

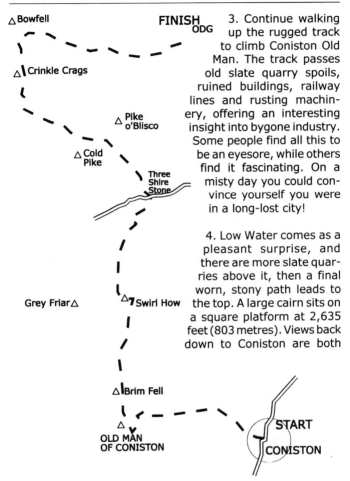

3. Continue walking up the rugged track to climb Coniston Old Man. The track passes old slate quarry spoils, ruined buildings, railway lines and rusting machinery, offering an interesting insight into bygone industry. Some people find all this to be an eyesore, while others find it fascinating. On a misty day you could convince yourself you were in a long-lost city!

4. Low Water comes as a pleasant surprise, and there are more slate quarries above it, then a final worn, stony path leads to the top. A large cairn sits on a square platform at 2,635 feet (803 metres). Views back down to Coniston are both

interesting and pleasant, but in the other direction lie range upon range of fine fells that delight the eye even more and promise a fine day's walk.

5. Simply follow a good path along the main crest of the Coniston Fells. There's a path junction where you keep right, and a slight gap is crossed on the way to Brim Fell. The broad

dome of Brim Fell is mostly grassy, but peppered with stones, bearing a cairn on top at 2,611 feet (795 metres). Beyond the summit the slope begins to fall more and more steeply, narrowing to become a rugged ridge.

6. A steep and stony path climbs up from a gap, then an easier path leads further along the crest to the prominent cairn on Swirl How at 2,637 feet (804 metres). The panorama seems more crowded with fells than from the Old Man and there's a good view across to Great Langdale where this walk is heading.

7. Leave Swirl How by walking west and gradually swing north around a rugged edge. Note a cairn just off to the left, where a piece of wreckage from a Halifax Bomber can be studied. The aircraft clipped the ridge in 1944, tearing off its undercarriage, and the rest of the wreckage fell over the edge. Follow the path to the summit of Great Carrs and admire the view before making a long descent.

8. The path is easy enough to follow as it continues northwards and gradually swings more north-east along a fairly well-defined ridge. However, keep an eye peeled for a small cairn where a path heads off to the left. This path zig-zags down and across a slope and eventually lands on a minor road at the top of the Wrynose Pass. Often, the pass is a jumble of haphazardly parked cars. In the middle of them all is a limestone pillar inscribed with the word 'Lancashire'. This is the Three Shire Stone, close to where the old counties of Lancashire, Westmorland and Cumberland met, until 1974.

9. Cross the road and follow another path uphill. It's a clear path that climbs to a broad gap where the little Red Tarn sits between Pike o' Blisco and Cold Pike. When a path junction is reached, notice the heavy bits of reddish haematite iron ore scattered around. If time is running out and a rapid descent to Langdale is required, then simply head straight onwards down into Oxendale to Stool End.

10. To continue with the high-level walk, however, turn left and follow a clear path up from the gap, across the slopes of Cold Fell and Great Knott. A rugged little summit is crossed on

the shoulder of Crinkle Crags, and beyond it is a rugged little gap. Notice how the path branches. The path to the left climbs up a steep and stony slope onto Crinkle Crags, while the one climbing more directly leads into a rocky gully where the only exit is by way of a short scramble. Either way aim to reach the summit of Crinkle Crags beyond at 2,816 feet (860 metres).

11. There's no doubt that the rocky crest of Crinkle Crags is a confusing place in poor visibility, and walkers have been known to describ complete circles! In clear weather, it's easy enough to look across all the humps and bumps and see the gap between the Crinkles and the proud face of Bowfell. The little pools known as the Three Tarns sit on this gap, though in very dry weather they can vanish entirely.

12. Turn right at the Three Tarns and pick up the pitched path leading down The Band. The slope quickly becomes quite gentle, then steepens again, with splendid views of the fells clustered around Great Langdale. At the very bottom of the slope, turn left and follow a track into the farmyard at Stool End. Simply walk along the farm access road to leave through the flat fields. At a road junction, a few paces lead to the point where the bus turns round near the Old Dungeon Ghyll Hotel before heading back to Ambleside.

Coniston Copper & Slate

Anyone with a particular interest in the old copper mines or slate quarries above Coniston should pay a visit to the enlarged and completely revamped Ruskin Museum in the village. Exhibits include a geological display as well as all sorts of other items related to the history and heritage of Coniston, including of course John Ruskin, who lived in the area from 1872 to 1900. The Ruskin Museum is tucked away in a secluded corner of the village but is signposted from the main street.

20

Coniston - Langdale - Elterwater - Grasmere

This is essentially a route that potters around the low fells and makes its way through wooded valleys from Coniston to Grasmere. It sounds like a long walk, but it's actually quite easy, and there's always the option of catching the bus from Elterwater after completing most of the route. Highlights include great views of the Coniston Fells, a walk beside a rocky gorge at Tilberthwaite, the lovely Little Langdale Tarn, the pretty little village of Elterwater, views of the Langdale Pikes and the verdant Vale of Grasmere. Buses to Coniston run from Ambleside and Ulverston. There are regular buses from Grasmere back to Ambleside.

Total distance: 10 miles (16 kilometres)
Height gain: 1,970 feet (600 metres)
Start: At the Black Bull in Coniston: GR302975
Finish: In the middle of Grasmere: GR337076

1. Coniston is a big village with plenty of shops and pubs if you need food and drink. The Black Bull stands beside a bridge in the middle of Coniston, and the road you follow out of the village runs between the Black Bull and the Co-op. The road is signposted for the Coppermines Youth Hostel, and it also passes the Ruskin Museum on its way out of the village. When the tarmac runs out, the road is firm and stony as it climbs up alongside Church Beck. The Miner's Bridge is reached, which spans a rocky gorge full of waterfalls, but don't cross over it.

2. Branch right up a stony track, then branch right again when a terrace of houses can be seen ahead. The track reaches another junction where you turn right yet again. Rise up a grassy ramp of a track, then at a cairn, turn left and follow a clear path rising across the fellside. Views across the

GRASMERE Coppermines Valley lead the eye to the higher fells. The path is generally buttressed on one side and leads through a little gap between Wetherlam and the Yewdale Fells.

Chapel Stile

Elterwater

3. Quarries and mines will have been noticed on the ascent, and there are more to see as the walk proceeds through the gap. Keep to the most obvious path running gently downhill and pass a couple of small quarried slits and a small stream on the way to Tilberthwaite. There's a wooded gorge on the descent, and as there are paths on both sides, you can choose which side you want to walk down. There's also a stepped path and footbridge halfway down that allows you to switch from one side to the other. Both paths land on a road at the bottom.

Little Langdale

High Tilberthwaite

4. Turn left and walk past Low Tilberthwaite, and notice its old spinning gallery, then continue along the road to walk though the farmyard at High Tilberthwaite. The tarmac ends and a firm, stony road leads through woodlands. Trees include birch, oak, alder, hawthorn and holly. Heaps of slate spoil are noticed, but stay on the most obvious road and don't follow tracks to left or right. The narrow road leads to a ford and footbridge over Little Langdale Beck, but don't cross over.

Coniston Fells

CONISTON START

5. Turn left and walk upstream a short way, though the track pulls away from the river as it rises. Turn right at a stile and gate and follow a path across the odd little stone arch called Slater's Bridge. A path continues straight uphill to Birk Howe Farm, with a fine view across Little Langdale Tarn to the higher fells. Follow the farm access road to a minor road. Turn left, then immediately right to continue up a clear, narrow road signed as 'unsuitable for motor vehicles'.

6. The road climbs to a farm, then a clear and obvious stony track continues through a gate and over a rise on the shoulder of Lingmoor Fell. The descent leads through another gate into woodland and the track is quite rough and stony in places. Follow a narrow road down to a minor road and turn left as signposted for Elterwater. The road crosses a bridge over Great Langdale Beck in the tiny village of Elterwater. There's a small shop and the Britannia Inn as well as a bus service.

7. To continue, follow the road out of Elterwater in the direction of Ambleside to reach a junction with the B5343 road serving Great Langdale. There's a lovely old milestone at the junction, as well as a fine view up the dale to the Langdale Pikes. Close to the junction you can find a path climbing straight up the bracken covered slopes of Elterwater Common. This leads up to another minor road and the ground can be wet underfoot.

8. Cross over the road and continue straight uphill, passing a little electricity substation concealed in the bracken. The path becomes dry and stony and leads onto a little gap in the fells, between Silver Howe and Red Bank. Although there is quite a network of paths, simply walk straight across the gap.

9. Drystone walls naturally funnel the path through a gate, then on the descent the path is confined to a wide strip of rough fellside bounded by drystone walls. Go down through another gate and enter Nicholas Wood, where a rough and cobbly track leads down to a road. At a junction, turn left to follow a minor road down towards Grasmere.

10. Buses stop beside the little green in the centre of the village, with frequent services to Keswick, Ambleside and Windermere.